ECHO

AND

CRITIQUE

ECHO
AND
CRITIQUE

POETRY
AND THE CLICHÉS OF
PUBLIC SPEECH

FLORIAN
GARGAILLO

LOUISIANA STATE
UNIVERSITY PRESS
BATON ROUGE

Published by Louisiana State University Press
lsupress.org

Designer: Andrew Shurtz
Typefaces: Garamond Premier Pro, Franklin Gothic URW

Library of Congress Cataloging-in-Publication Data

Names: Gargaillo, Florian, author.
Title: Echo and critique : poetry and the clichés of public speech /
    Florian Gargaillo.
Description: Baton Rouge : Louisiana State University Press, [2023] |
    Includes bibliographical references and index.
Identifiers: LCCN 2022042821 (print) | LCCN 2022042822 (ebook) |
    ISBN 978-0-8071-7935-2 (cloth) | ISBN 978-0-8071-7999-4 (epub) |
    ISBN 978-0-8071-8000-6 (pdf)
Subjects: LCSH: American poetry—20th century—History and
    criticism. | Clichés in literature. | Politics and literature—United
    States—History—20th century. | United States—Intellectual
    life—20th century. | LCGFT: Literary criticism.
Classification: LCC PS310.C59 G37 2023 (print) | LCC PS310.C59
    (ebook) | DDC 811/.509—dc23/eng/20230227
LC record available at https://lccn.loc.gov/2022042821
LC ebook record available at https://lccn.loc.gov/2022042822

CONTENTS

ECHO

AND

CRITIQUE

INTRODUCTION

This book tells the story of how poets in the United States came to apprehend, critically, the clichés of public discourse in the wake of World War II. During this period, public intellectuals of various stripes—working in fields as diverse as journalism, political science, sociology, linguistics, history, and literary criticism—arrived at a grim verdict. Political discourse, they said, had become saturated with abstract stock phrases that euphemize, obscure, and evade. While clichés in public speech are hardly a new phenomenon, the consensus was that these phrases had grown both more numerous and more sinister, as they were now being used to silence dissent, excuse corruption, and disguise atrocities. Poets who shared these concerns developed a distinctive method, which I call "echo and critique," to confront political cant head-on. A poet making use of echo and critique would quote a stock phrase from public discourse and then draw on various poetic tools in the line's context (from imagery to meter and rhyme) to reveal its implications, identify the values it promotes, and weigh its effects. This method could be found in poetry associated with vastly different groups, from the Auden circle and the Harlem Renaissance, to Confessional Poetry, the New York School, and the Beats, making it an important feature of contemporary writing. And it continues to be used today. Yet echo and critique has gone unnoticed, despite its continued relevance in the twenty-first century. This book, in uncovering the forgotten history of echo and critique, shows how poetry can help us better examine the cant that is everywhere in public speech, so we may not be controlled by it.

The stock phrases that so preoccupied the intellectuals of the postwar era were referred to under various names, including "cant" (the jargon of a particular group, especially a professional class); "bureaucratese" (the official-sounding language of governments designed to exude authority);

"doublespeak" (euphemisms that obscure reality by seeming to say the opposite of what they mean); and "weasel words" (terms that sound specific but are in fact vague and abstract), to name a few examples. While each of these terms carries a different shade of meaning, all fall under the banner of "cliché" and share some key traits. A cliché is typically assumed to have been around too long and lack originality. It is, according to the *Oxford English Dictionary*, "a phrase or expression regarded as unoriginal or trite due to overuse." But in the context of public rhetoric, this definition warrants qualification. Some political clichés of the period were indeed old phrases put to new purposes, like "Collective Man." Still others, like "streamline operations" (instead of "laying off employees"), were freshly minted by bureaucracies and communications offices. What made these various phrases clichés was not so much their overuse, or not simply that, but rather the mindlessness with which they were deployed or received. A political cliché is a phrase doled out from habit, a phrase intended to discourage the listener from critical thinking, or both. Indeed, it was the absence or suppression of thought that concerned midcentury intellectuals most deeply. This thread runs through writers as varied as George Orwell, Hannah Arendt, and Lionel Trilling. It unites phrases as diverse as the resonant slogans of World War II propaganda and the numbing jargon of bureaucratese. Overuse was merely a symptom of the speaker's inanity, or (more darkly) a technique used to dissuade the public from scrutinizing the words too critically.

Perhaps the most famous statement about political clichés in this period is George Orwell's "Politics and the English Language." First published in *Horizon* in April 1946, the essay became a cornerstone for other commentators of the postwar era. To Orwell, political discourse had become so saturated with clichés that the stock phrase was now the basic building block of all sentences in the public sphere: "As soon as certain topics are raised, the concrete melts into the abstract and no one seems able to think of turns of speech that are not hackneyed: prose consists less and less of *words* chosen for the sake of their meaning, and more and more of phrases tacked together like the sections of a prefabricated henhouse."[1] The appeal of these *phrases* lies precisely in the fact that they are easy to use, like "a packet of aspirins always at one's elbow."[2] By removing the effort needed for clear, meaningful communication, clichés dissuade both speaker and audience from exercising critical thought: "If thought corrupts language, language can also corrupt thought. A bad usage can spread by tradition and imitation even among people who should and do know better."[3] The speaker who relies on clichés becomes, in Orwell's description, akin to a machine:

> When one watches some tired hack on the platform mechanically repeating the familiar phrases—*bestial atrocities, iron heel, blood-stained tyranny, free peoples of the world, stand shoulder to shoulder*—one often has a curious feeling that one is not watching a live human being but some kind of dummy: a feeling which suddenly becomes stronger at moments when the light catches the speaker's spectacles and turns them into blank discs which seem to have no eyes behind them. . . . A speaker who uses that kind of phraseology has gone some distance toward turning himself into a machine. The appropriate noises are coming out of his larynx, but his brain is not involved as it would be if he were choosing his words for himself.[4]

Writing a year after World War II, Orwell recognized yet another risk with political stock phrases. Not only could clichés dress up an empty statement and make it appear meaningful, but they could also defend the indefensible and disguise atrocities. Several of the examples that he cites are drawn from the dictatorships of Germany and Italy, which had developed a sophisticated set of terms to "package" their cruelest practices:

> Defenseless villages are bombarded from the air, the inhabitants driven out into the countryside, the cattle machine-gunned, the huts set on fire with incendiary bullets: this is called *pacification*. Millions of peasants are robbed of their farms and sent trudging along the roads with no more than they can carry: this is called *transfer of population* or *rectification of frontiers*. People are imprisoned for years without trial, or shot in the back of the neck or sent to die of scurvy in Arctic lumber camps: this is called *elimination of unreliable elements*.[5]

Thus, Orwell's insistence on pressing back against clichés was motivated not by a belief in linguistic purity but by fear of what the abuse of language might conceal and enable. Moreover, Orwell knew that this phenomenon was not limited to dictatorships: it was a rhetorical feature of democracies as well.

Orwell was just one of many who lamented the state of public discourse after World War II. Indeed, this idea was so pervasive that it is worth considering a few notable examples from different corners of the American public sphere to show its reach. Three years after "Politics and the English Language," Lionel Trilling published an essay titled "The Meaning of a Literary Idea" in which he argued that the spread of abstraction threatened the ability not only to talk about emotion, but even to feel at all:

> A specter haunts our culture—it is that people will eventually be unable to say, "They fell in love and married," let alone understand the language of *Romeo and Juliet*, but will as a matter of course say, "Their libidinal impulses being reciprocal, they activated their individual erotic drives and integrated them within the same frame of reference." Now this is not the language of abstract thought or of any kind of thought. It is the language of non-thought. But it is the language which is developing from the peculiar status which we in our culture have given to abstract thought. There can be no doubt whatever that it constitutes a threat to the emotions and thus to life itself.[6]

To Hannah Arendt, political clichés had deep roots in dictatorial regimes. In *Eichmann in Jerusalem: A Report on the Banality of Evil* (1963), a study of one of the organizers of the Holocaust, she identified the cliché as the defining feature of totalitarian thought. Eichmann's wholehearted embrace of *officialese* had made it possible for him to ignore other points of view and repress sympathy for the victims of the Third Reich. Thus, Arendt drew a direct line from Eichmann's reliance on stock phrases to the atrocities that he brought about:

> The point here is that officialese became his language because he was genuinely incapable of uttering a single sentence that was not a cliché. . . . The longer one listened to him, the more obvious it

became that his inability to speak was closely connected with an inability to think, namely to think from the standpoint of somebody else. No communication was possible with him, not because he lied but because he was surrounded by the most reliable of all safeguards against the words and the presence of others, and hence against reality as such.[7]

Not that these habits were limited to dictatorships. Herbert Marcuse, in *One-Dimensional Man* (1964), argued that tautologies dominated the public discourse of democratic societies, too. In formulating his argument, Marcuse acknowledged a debt to Orwell but stressed that the history of doublespeak stretched further back: "That a political party which works for the defense and growth of capitalism is called 'Socialist,' and a despotic government 'democratic,' and a rigged election 'free' are familiar linguistic—and political—features which long predate Orwell."[8] What made the tautologies of his own decade distinct was the queasy union of politics and advertising: "Total commercialization joins formerly antagonistic spheres of life, and this union expresses itself in the smooth linguistic conjunction of conflicting parts of speech. To a mind not yet sufficiently conditioned, much of the public speaking and printing appears utterly surrealistic. Captions such as 'Labor is Seeking Missile Harmony,' and advertisements such as 'Luxury Fall-Out Shelter' may still evoke the naïve reaction that 'Labor,' 'Missile,' and 'Harmony' are irreconcilable contradiction, and that no logic and no language should be capable of correctly joining luxury and fall-out."[9] In the field of linguistics, the issue of political doublespeak was taken up most notably by Mario Pei, who published two books on the subject: *Words in Sheep's Clothing* (1969) and *Doublespeak in America* (1973). To Pei, the real threat came from what he termed "weasel words." These were "used and misused not through habit, inadvertence, or accident, but coined or distorted, and then put into circulation by deliberate design, for purposes of deception." Like many of his contemporaries, Pei framed this as a distinctly contemporary issue. He wrote of "weasel words" in his own era: "a new and bountiful crop has sprung up."[10]

Poets played an important role in the debate around this problem. At times, they sniffed out in each other's work the same linguistic phenomenon that was present across the public sphere. One notorious instance of this was Randall Jarell's harsh assessment of W. H. Auden and the style that he adopted in the 1930s. In the essay "Changes of Attitude and Rhetoric in Auden's Poetry" (1941), Jarrell accused Auden of relying too much on abstract phrases. The language of his recent poems, he argued, was "relatively passive and abstract; full of adverbs, adjectives, intransitive verbs"; it seemed "pale and feeble by the side of his magnificently verb-y early speech."[11] In one striking passage, Jarrell bought an overwhelming slew of examples to bear as evidence:

> There is a thirteen-line menagerie where I Will, I Know, I Am, I Have Not, and I Am Loved peer idiotically from behind their bars; nearby, gobbling peanuts, throng the Brothered-One, the Not-Alone, the Just, the Happy-Go-Lucky, the Filthy, hundreds of We's and They's and Their's and Our's and Me's, the Terrible Demon, the Lost People, the Great, the Old Masters, and the Unexpected; they feel Love and Hate and Lust and Things; above them hover all sorts of tutelary deities: the Present, the Past, the Future, the Just City, the Good Place, Fate, Pride, Charity, Success, Knowledge, Wisdom, Violence, Life and Art and Salvation and Matter and the Nightmare, Form, the State, Democracy, Authority, Duality, Business, Collective Man, the Generalized Life, the Meaning of Knowing, the Flower of the Ages, and Real Estate. Reading *Another Time* is like attending an Elks' Convention of the Capitalized Letters; all my examples come from it, and I had not even begun to exhaust the supply.[12]

Jarrell spoke of his attraction to stock phrases as a form of dependence. Using language that closely echoed Orwell's line about "aspirins always at one's elbow," he described rhetorical phrases as an addictive substance: "The terrible thing about such rhetorical devices, about any of the mechanisms and patented insights that make up so much of any style, is that they are habit-forming, something the style demands in ever-increasing quantities."[13] In Jarrell's account, Auden has become akin to the public speaker imagined by Orwell, his spectacles having turned to "blank discs which seem to have no eyes behind them." He dishes abstract phrases out mechanically and finds that he resorts to them more and more as time goes by. In effect, he has ceased to think critically about his own use of language, in addition to public discourse.

The passages quoted here represent just a small sample of a much larger conversation about political clichés that took place from the start of the Second World War to the end of the Vietnam War. Of course, it is important to note that the use of stock phrases in public discourse was not itself new. William Lutz points out anecdotally: "When traitors were put to death in Rome, the announcement of their execution was made in the form of saying 'they have lived.' 'Taking notice of a man in the ancestral manner' meant capital punishment; 'the prisoner was then led away' meant he was executed."[14] Nor did objections to political clichés begin in 1939. Handwringing on the subject extends much further back. In 1720, Jonathan Swift issued a similar complaint about the use of professional jargon to obfuscate and impress rather than to communicate:

> I know not how it comes to pass, that professors in most arts and sciences are generally the worst qualified to explain their meanings to those who are not of their tribe: a common farmer shall make you understand in three words, that *his foot is out of joint*, or *his collar-bone broken*, wherein a surgeon, after a hundred terms of art, if you are not a scholar, shall leave you to seek. It is frequently the same case in law, physic, and even many of the meaner arts.[15]

In *Rights of Man* (1791), Thomas Paine lamented the vacuity of political discourse in England. To his mind, the word "Constitution" had been emptied of meaning and become a "cant word" which the political class turned to thoughtlessly out of habit:

> The continual use of the word *Constitution* in the English Parliament, shews there is none; and that the whole is merely a form of Government without a Constitution, and constituting itself with what powers it pleases. If there were a Constitution, it certainly could be referred to; and the debate on any constitutional point, would terminate by producing the Constitution. One member says, This is Constitution; and another says, That is Constitution—To-day

it is one thing; and to-morrow, it is something else—while the maintaining of the debate proves there is none. Constitution is now the cant word of Parliament, tuning itself to the ear of the Nation.[16]

Poets have long partaken in this critique as well. Lord Byron, writing to John Murray in 1821, railed against "Cant political—Cant poetical—Cant religious—Cant moral," which he deemed the *"primum mobile"* of English life.[17]

Still, these anxieties took on a much greater force after 1939, and there are several historical reasons for that shift. First, as the Orwell and Arendt examples make clear, the totalitarian regimes in place during World War II supplied copious examples of clichés being used or even fabricated to conceal atrocities. The risk posed by political stock phrases was simply more apparent coming after "transfer of population" and "elimination of unreliable elements." Thus, pushing back against cant became not just a matter of resisting emptiness in public discourse but also exposing political corruption and safeguarding democracy. The second reason for the increased skepticism toward clichés has to do with mass media. During the war, radio surpassed the newspaper as the primary source of news in the United States.[18] This altered the relation between public communication and its audience. The problem of cant simply took on far greater immediacy in a context where the voice of the state and the country's political parties could speak to you directly in your home. At the same time, the nature of radio led to profound changes in the nature and quality of public discourse itself. Whereas a newspaper allows readers to go back and reread particular sentences, a radio program does not offer the luxury of "listening back." Consequently, scriptwriters, as well as political speechwriters and public communications offices, had to ensure that they could convey their messages simply and efficiently. Mitchell Charnley's *News by Radio* (1948), a guide for aspiring journalists, shows the impact of this change in his description of good newsroom practice:

Radio news is essentially plain, straight talk.

In the normal flow of a news broadcast, each item is stated only once. The listener has no chance of rehearing, or of referring to the script, so the following challenges confront the writer and announcer:

1. The news must be kept alive to command the listener's attention throughout.
2. The script must be more than factually correct; its wording must be so clear-cut that the listener understands exactly in one telling.[19]

This new world of communications increased pressure on politicians, governments, and businesses to develop a ready-made, formalized vocabulary that could be deployed efficiently in the new media to defend and promote their actions. The abstract stock phrases that were used as a result, from "free enterprise" to "revenue enhancement," were useful because they gave the illusion of a clear statement while simplifying (the first example), obfuscating (the second), or distorting reality (in both). Indeed, the fact that audiences could not listen back became an asset—one that would carry over with the rise of television, another medium that required efficient communication, in the 1950s and 1960s.

Echo and critique—the method that poets developed to analyze stock phrases critically—was capacious and flexible enough to take on clichés of various stripes, from the slogans of wartime propaganda to the convoluted jargon of bureaucracy. Simply put, a poet performing echo and critique would quote a cliché from public discourse and then use the line's surrounding context to gloss its meaning (or expose its lack of meaning), unpack its implications, identify its limitations, and consider its effects. To analyze stock phrases, poets used a variety of the techniques from their toolbox, including rhyme, alliteration, assonance, meter, simile, and metaphor. Poetry, more than fiction or drama, was especially well suited to this mode of close listening, thanks to its heightened attentiveness to linguistic particulars. An artform where every verbal detail matters profoundly, from word choice and punctuation to line structure, could apply a high degree of critical pressure to the phrases that it takes up.

When looking at instances of echo and critique, the relationship between poetry and public discourse can be framed in terms of the relationship between counterpublics and dominant publics. As Michael Warner has famously argued, public discourse "promises to address anybody" and in so doing speaks to us not as individuals but as part of a group of "indefinite others."[20] Yet even as they claim to offer a formal, abstract, universalizing vocabulary with which to discuss matters of public interest, readymade phrases maintain a divide between the insiders who formulate the phrases (the politician or the political class, the state bureaucracy, and the corporate office) and the outsiders subject to them. Counterpublics offer an alternative to these dominant discourses; they also prompt a different understanding of audience. From Warner again: "Like all publics, a counterpublic comes into being through an address to indefinite strangers. . . . But counterpublic discourse also addresses those strangers as being not just anybody. Addressees are socially marked by their participation in this kind of discourse."[21] When they make use of echo and critique, poets do not conceive of their audience or public as a totalizing collective. Poetry's marginal status precludes that assumption. They do, however, address a subset of "indefinite strangers": readers of poetry who long for an individual, skeptical counterpoint to the omniscient and impersonal voice of public discourse.

At this juncture, I would like to unpack the term I designed for this method and explain the reasoning behind each of the key words that constitute it. "Echo" is an appropriate word for two reasons. First, it evokes the mythical story of Narcissus and in doing so captures one of the principal accusations leveled against political cant: namely, that it is a self-serving, solipsistic form of speech. Second, it reflects the ambiguous provenance of the phrases. While some clichés of public discourse can be traced back to a single point (like Franklin Roosevelt's "Four Freedoms"), many more do not have a discernible origin (like "strategic initiatives"). The advantage of a word like "echo" is that it preserves this ambiguity. "Quote" would imply that the author can be identified, but the source of an "echo" can be known or unknown.

"Critique" may seem like a curious choice in light of recent debates surrounding that word, particularly since Rita Felski's *The Limits of Critique* (2015). In that book, Felski argues that the academic overreliance on the term "critique" betrays an assumption that texts conceal meaning and that a responsible scholar must approach the text with suspicion, ready to uncover what it obscures. Instead, Felski proposes that critics position themselves "in front of the text, reflecting on what it unfurls, calls forth, makes possible."[22] Although I use various terms in the book to describe how poets respond to political clichés (such as "analyze" and "examine"), I opted for "critique" for the central term because the "hermeneutics of suspicion" Felski attributes to literary critics is in fact the dominant mode of poetry's relationship to cant. By echoing stock phrases from public discourse, poets operate from the belief that political clichés, no matter how mindlessly they are deployed, carry with them buried ideas and messages for the poet to uncover. In sum, this book does not enter into recent debates about reading, but it does show that critique—which has come under increasing pressure in how literary scholars think about their work— defined and continues to define how poets respond to political cant.

The most important precursor to echo and critique at the start of the twentieth century was Robert Frost. Unlike his modernist contemporaries, who sought to either defamiliarize language or "purify the dialect of the tribe,"[23] Frost felt that poetry should closely emulate ordinary language. In this regard, he can be seen as descending from poets of previous centuries who advocated for a return to "the language of common men" (William Wordsworth being a key figure).[24] What set Frost apart from these predecessors, and reflected a distinctly modern sensibility, was his skepticism toward popular aphorisms that enabled, and perhaps even fostered, a narrow view of complex realities. His poetry contains several instances of him echoing popular sayings in order to then demonstrate their limits. Perhaps the most well-known example of this appears in "Mending Wall." The speaker of that poem describes his encounters with a neighbor who insists on building a wall between their two lands, though it will serve little practical use: "My apple trees will never get across / And eat the cones under his pines, I tell him."[25] Despite this, the neighbor always repeats the phrase: "Good fences make good neighbors." To Frost's ear, aphorisms operate as verbal security blankets, asserting the speaker's position while saving them the effort of justifying or examining their beliefs. The phrase appears twice in the poem; in both instances, the poet frames it to emphasize its impoverished thinking: "He *only* says," (my emphasis), "He will not go behind his father's saying, / And he likes having thought of it so well / he says again." In sum, even as Frost celebrated ordinary language in poetry, he also showed considerable resistance to aphorisms, which he felt reflected a tendency to rely on ready-made ideas instead of thinking actively through language.

That said, Frost rarely turned his ear to the ready-made phrases of public discourse, preferring instead to focus on the language of ordinary people. The first to devote his attention to the proliferation of bureaucratese and other political clichés in the public sphere was W. H. Auden, whose artistic coming-of-age coincided with the historical forces I have previously described. He is also the first to methodically take apart the linguistic particulars of these phrases. Even though Frost was critical of the popular sayings he echoed and wrote of their limitations, he did not examine closely the linguistic details that make up a given phrase. Auden was the first to not just be critical of clichés but to really critique them by scrutinizing individual words and structures using a variety of poetic tools, including rhyme, meter, metaphor, and structure. In this regard, he can be considered the founder of echo and critique, to the extent that this method can be ascribed to a single point of origin.

Auden's popularity and influence in the 1930s and 1940s made it possible for echo and critique to get picked up by a wide variety of poets, first among traditional formalists working closely with Auden, and then out to writers associated formerly with the Harlem Renaissance, to Confessional poets, the New York School, and the Beats. Moreover, echo and critique is still widely used today. As an example of how this method works, and proof of its continued relevance in the twenty-first century, consider the following lines from "In Montgomery" (2003) by Gwendolyn Brooks.

> In Montgomery is no Race Problem.
> There is the white decision, the white and pleasant vow
> that the white foot shall not release the Black neck.[26]

The poem focuses in on the phrase "Race Problem," here capitalized to emphasize that it is a bit of borrowed language. Brooks's main objection is that "race problem" obscures the reality of racism in America: by refusing to name and distinguish between groups, the phrase implies that responsibility might be shared equally by all. The lines that follow explicitly distinguish "white" and "Black," and show that the country's so-called "Race Problem" is actually a problem of white people inflicting violence against Black people. The poem makes that reality harder to ignore in this poem thanks to the repetition of the word "white" in "the white decision," "the white and pleasant vow," and "the white foot." By expanding the word's reach across two lines, Brooks evokes the experience of living in a society where one group occupies a dominant position. At the same time, the capitalization of the word "Black" at the end of the third line takes on a special function in this context, by pushing back against the spatial, musical, and metaphorical pressure that "white" has accumulated up to now. Brooks's poem is a prime example of echo and critique thanks to the multiplicity of tools that it uses to expand on the implications of a given phrase and identify its limits.

To get a sharper sense of the parameters and characteristics of echo and critique, it is worth considering how this method differs from others that might seem to be in the same neighborhood. Echo and critique is, importantly, not pastiche, in that the poet does not imitate the various linguistic patterns of a given discourse (tone, vocabulary, syntax, etc.) across an entire poem. Instead, a poet who makes use of echo and critique will select a single phrase or a narrow set of phrases to examine in depth. The force of the poet's analysis depends on the contrast between the cliché and its context, which markedly does not belong to the same discourse. By pitting a stock phrase against their own voice, poets make the cliché unfamiliar again, so that they (and we) may examine it afresh.

A similar distinction can be drawn between echo and critique and more recent experiments like Kenneth Goldsmith's "uncreative writing." Goldsmith typically takes large swaths of language from a genre or event (be it a traffic report or live television coverage of Michael Jackson's death) and then transcribes and rearranges that text into what he calls a poem. His idiosyncratic method, descended from pastiche, is inspired by a sense of linguistic saturation. For Goldsmith, media has dominated public life so completely that it is now impossible to say anything original. The most a poet can do is take what has already been said and then reorganize that language so that it can be seen in a new light. As he writes in the introduction to *Uncreative Writing:* "It seems an appropriate response to a new condition in writing today: faced with an unprecedented amount of available text, the problem is not needing to write more of it; instead, we must learn to negotiate the vast quantity that exists. How I make my way through this thicket of information—how I manage it, how I parse it, how I organize and distribute it—is what distinguishes my writing from yours."[27] Two important differences emerge here between Goldsmith's approach and echo and critique. First, whereas Goldsmith responds to the saturation of new media as reflected in an "unprecedented amount of available text," echo and critique is a rebuttal to the perceived corruption of public discourse by clichés. Second, Goldsmith sees his role as archival rather than critical. Granted, he does not go so far as to describe his work as wholly neutral, since rearranging a text into a new collage does require him to make choices (selecting the language, deciding how to structure it and lay it out on the page). But his stated goal is simply to present existing language, not to examine it critically as in echo and critique. For instance, consider the following lines from *Seven American Deaths and Disasters,* in which Goldsmith transcribes and rearranges a news report covering the attacks on the World Trade Center.

> This just in. You are looking at obviously a very disturbing live shot here. That is the World Trade Center, and we have unconfirmed reports this morning that a plane has crashed into one of the towers of the World Trade Center.
>
> We are right now just beginning to work on this story, obviously calling our sources and trying to figure out exactly what happened. But clearly, something relatively devastating happening this morning here on the south end of the island of Manhattan.
>
> This is, once again, a picture of one of the towers of the World Trade Center.[28]

There would be room here for a critical response to the language of live news reporting. The word "relatively" (a filler word) is painfully unsuitable in this context, as the World Trade Center attacks were far worse than "relatively" devastating. Yet the most that Goldsmith's method does is reveal how strange the first reactions to 9/11 sound when heard from a historical distance: how little they knew then and how much we know now. His aim is not to examine the emptiness of TV news talk, nor to criticize it for being careless or out of touch, but simply to draw out its features in a bolder fashion. The purpose of echo and critique, by contrast, is to analyze and evaluate.

By tracing a popular yet little-discussed model used by poets to apprehend political cant, this book enters into a very old debate about the relationship between poetry and cliché. It has long been said that poets who do not merely succumb to clichés will seek to renew them. Donald Davie, in *Purity of Diction in English Verse* (1967), celebrated the capacity of poetry to "revivify metaphors gone dead": "For if the poet who coins new metaphors *enlarges* the language, the poet who enlivens dead metaphors can be said to *purify* the language."[29] Christopher Ricks later contended that, "instead of banishing or shunning clichés as malign," poets ought "to meet them imaginatively, to create benign possibilities for and with them." The key lay in "using clichés . . . not being used by them."[30] Over the decades, critics have praised specific writers for taking up this challenge successfully. Jonathan Culler has commended Charles Baudelaire's skills in "reanimating" clichés.[31] For Edna Longley, the power of Paul Muldoon's writing comes, at least in part, from the way that he "restores full significance to more abstract phrases."[32] John Shoptaw has also identified as one of John Ashbery's chief traits the "recycling" of "stock phrases, figures, and meanings."[33]

Echo and critique differs from this model in important ways. Poets who made use of echo and critique did not seek to restore or renew the clichés of public speech. Instead, their aim was to renew our attention to political clichés and help us to view them critically, so that we might better understand and control them. The difference between echo and critique and this other model stems from the nature of the specific phrases that poets responded to in each case. Generally speaking, the clichés that critics have focused on are drawn from ordinary language: namely, mundane idioms like "in the nick of time" or "scared to death." By contrast, the stock phrases that poets examined using echo and critique were drawn from the official discourse of politicians, state bureaucracies, and corporations, divorced from everyday language. These phrases were used not by ordinary people but by those in power to solidify and expand their grasp. As such, they required a different, more skeptical response, because the threat that they posed to a healthy democracy were far greater.

Echo and Critique traces the history of this method over four decades, from the start of World War II to the end of the Vietnam War. Each chapter focuses on a representative poet and the work they produced during a specific timeframe within that broader postwar period. The poets discussed here were selected, first and foremost, because they made use of echo and critique particularly often, and thus showed a sustained interest in the possibilities of this method. Some also mark important turning points in how poets understood political clichés. Josephine Miles, for example, was one of the first poets to extensively consider the infiltration of business talk into every corner of public discourse, including politics. Lastly, the poets selected for inclusion here have a distinctively complex relation to political clichés, which impacted their writing and how they understood their position in society. For instance, several were conscious of the proximity between their own style and the genre of public discourse they wished to push back against. Robert Lowell acknowledged his attraction to political oratory even as he objected to the stock phrases of Lyndon Johnson's presidential speeches. Randall Jarrell recognized the inevitability of using abstraction in war poetry at the same time that he recoiled from abstract phrases in war propaganda. As a result, their use of echo and critique fostered a more critical relationship with their own writing. More broadly, they recognized the susceptibility of all writers, speakers, and citizens to the clichés of public speech. Even though they are designed by politicians, government entities, and corporations, political clichés easily make their way into everyday discourse. Thus, whatever polemical or didactic qualities the poems contain are balanced by an alertness to that risk. What Willard Spiegelman has said about the poetry of instruction after World War II applies here: "the pedagogy is inflected with irony, wit, self-deprecation, and skepticism."[34]

This history of echo and critique begins with a chapter on W. H. Auden, who more than anyone can be credited for popularizing this method at the turn of the 1940s. In his earliest poems, and most notoriously in "Spain," Auden tended to simply absorb and leverage stock phrases in the service of his chosen political causes. His move to the United States in the late 1930s marked an important shift, however, as he began to examine critically the idioms of bureaucratese that he felt had gained a foothold in public speech.

I then turn to a series of chapters on poetry written during World War II, when a host of new and refurbished stock phrases were aired out to galvanize support for the Allied troops. The first of these chapters focuses on Randall Jarrell, who critiqued the clichés of war propaganda (in particular abstract phrases centered around terms of value like "freedom" and "justice") to reveal the distance of that language from the experience of soldiers fighting in the war. Langston Hughes, the subject of the following chapter, was also struck by the gap between rhetoric and reality, but the more pressing issue for him was the dissonance between America's claim that it was fighting for freedom abroad and the fact that the United States continued to deprive many of its own citizens of freedom on the basis of race. Claude McKay, the last author discussed in this section, is notable for using echo and critique to analyze the language of domestic conflicts, especially on the subject of class and race. His poems are thus an important record of what was said "on the home front" during the war, and how some poets responded to the public discourse on domestic issues.

The period covered in the next three chapters, from 1960 to 1975, presents a radically different moment in American politics and so engendered a very different response from its poets. This era witnessed growing concerns about America's role in the world as a global superpower, as well as the persistence of inequality within its borders. Robert Lowell, who had declared himself a conscientious objector in World War II and now came out against America's actions in the Vietnam War, focused his echo and critique on the presidential speeches of Lyndon Johnson. These, he felt, revealed the decline of American political rhetoric, for they were written by public communication specialists tasked with shielding the president from criticism, while allowing institutions to continue the exercise (and abuse) of power. During the same period, Josephine Miles detected a shift in public discourse: the permeation of business talk into every area of public life, including politics. For her, the real center of power lay increasingly in the hands of global corporations, which set the terms—in a contractual and linguistic sense—of international relations. The last poet in this section, Seamus Heaney, considered another important change: the infiltration of the worst traits in public rhetoric (evasion, abstraction) into everyday conversation about public events. While living and teaching in California, Heaney reflected on the day-to-day talk he heard about the Irish Troubles at home, and examined the way that politicians and television reports had shaped, and distorted, how ordinary people thought and talked about the conflict. In sum, Heaney matters to the history of echo and critique because he showed, more fully than any poet before him, the threat that political clichés posed to ordinary language.

Echo and critique did not end in 1975, but that year does provide a useful stopping point, since it marked the end of the Vietnam War, a conflict that spurred a widespread debate about the problems and limitations of public speech. The method, which Auden first popularized and which generations of poets took up in turn, is still alive and well in our own moment. This book offers a history of its formative decades, as well as a map for identifying its use in the poetry of the present and future. More broadly, the goal of this study is to delineate one important way that poetry can help us navigate public speech and understand the clichés that lay claim to us, so that we may view them critically and not be possessed by them.

1

W. H. AUDEN
ON
BUREAUCRATESE

W. H. Auden was not the first poet to scrutinize political clichés in his writing, but he was the first to make it central to his poetic practice. Auden came to echo and critique gradually over a three-year period, from 1937 to 1940. His widespread influence throughout the following decade—during what many termed "the age of Auden"[1]—led other writers to adopt this method in turn, so that Auden became the chief popularizer of echo and critique in the 1940s.

It may seem paradoxical, then, that Auden has also been accused of succumbing to clichés in his own writing. Randall Jarrell, in a 1941 essay for the *Southern Review,* vigorously attacked Auden for relying too much on "capitalized personified abstractions" akin to the impersonal lingo of state bureaucracies, such as "Collective Man, the Generalized Life, the Meaning of Knowing, the Flower of the Ages."[2] Jarrell was troubled by the phrases because Auden did not appear to be in control of them; they had become "habit-forming, something the style demands in ever-increasing quantities."[3] That reflexive use was what made the phrases clichés in his mind, whether they were in fact widely used in public discourse (like "Collective Man") or of the poet's own coinage (like "the Generalized Life," which sounds like—but was not in fact—a stock phrase). Moreover, Jarrell's reproaches still haunt Auden today. R. Clifton Spargo, following Jarrell's lead, writes that "as Auden had moved increasingly toward a language of abstraction, he had sought to make himself more accessible and to oppose the obscurity of the modernists, but the result of his experiment had been to mystify many of the social forces of which he had previously been so critical and to settle for a rhetoric of bureaucratic depersonalization."[4]

These criticisms are not wholly unfair. At the start of his career, Auden was certainly drawn to abstract phrases for their rhetorical force. It is also true that, throughout the early and mid-1930s, he tended to ride on the immediate effect of these phrases instead of examining them critically (the most notorious example being the poem "Spain"). But the end of that decade marked an important shift that Jarrell did not acknowledge, as Auden grew conscious of his own susceptibility to the very rhetorical mechanisms that he deplored in the public sphere. Echoing and critiquing stock phrases from political discourse enabled him to get a purchase on his own use of abstraction, by developing a more critical approach to clichés that he could then apply to his writing. At the same time, Auden did not believe that it was possible to rid oneself of clichés entirely. As Patrick Deer has noted, he acknowledged "the twists and turns required to challenge official rhetoric and the tenacious grip of the war-makers over language."[5] His tendency to fall back into old habits made it clear how difficult it is to speak of social and political matters without resorting to abstract stock phrases as well. Thus, the late 1930s was the period in which Auden came to terms with both his own failings and the risks inherent to public discourse, while honing a method that would leave a permanent mark on poetic history.

The poem that revealed to Auden the danger of abstract phrases and his own susceptibility to them was "Spain." Auden had traveled to the country in January 1937, in the thick of the Spanish Civil War, to support the Republicans in their fight against General Francisco Franco. Although he had originally intended to drive an ambulance, he found a job in propaganda broadcasting instead. Little is known about the specific tasks he performed, but after seven weeks he returned to England, disillusioned by the violence he had witnessed on the Republican side.[6] Despite this, he continued to voice his support for the cause. In May, he released a pamphlet through Faber and Faber titled *Spain,* in which he defended the uprising in terms that soon proved controversial.

The titular poem "Spain" works largely by repetition and contrast, weighing the sacrifices that must be endured "to-day" against the promise of a happy future "to-morrow." In the twenty-fourth stanza (of twenty-six), Auden writes:

> To-day the deliberate increase in the chances of death,
> The conscious acceptance of guilt in the necessary murder;
> To-day the expending of powers
> On the flat ephemeral pamphlet and the boring meeting.[7]

George Orwell notoriously criticized the second line as a symptom of Auden's detachment from the realities of war. In the essay titled "Political Reflections on the Crisis," published in the *Adelphi* in December 1938, he wrote pointedly, "Mr. Auden can write about 'the acceptance of guilt for the necessary murder' because he has never committed a murder, perhaps never had one of his friends murdered, possibly never even seen a murdered man's corpse."[8] Two years later, in the 1940 essay "Inside the Whale," Orwell expanded on this criticism by zeroing in on a phrase:

> Notice the phrase "necessary murder." It could only be written by a person to whom murder is at most a *word*. Personally I would not speak so lightly of murder. It so happens that I have seen the bodies of numbers of murdered men—I don't mean killed in battle, I mean murdered. Therefore I have some conception of what murder means—the terror, the hatred, the howling relatives, the post-mortems, the blood, the smells. To me, murder is something to be avoided. So it is to any ordinary person. The Hitlers and Stalins find murder necessary, but they don't advertise their callousness, and they don't speak of it as murder; it is "liquidation," "elimination," or some other soothing phrase. Mr. Auden's brand of amoralism is only possible, if you are the kind of person who is always somewhere else when the trigger is pulled. So much of left-wing thought is a kind of playing with fire by people who don't even know that fire is hot. The warmongering to which the English intelligentsia gave themselves up in the period 1935–39 was largely based on a sense of personal immunity.[9]

The lines in which Orwell identifies the "soothing phrases" doled out by dictators contains the seeds of his 1946 essay "Politics and the English Language," with its analysis of euphemistic doublespeak: "Political language . . . is designed to make lies sound truthful and murder respectable, and to give an appearance of solidity to pure wind."[10] By this date, writing in the aftermath of World War II, Orwell had come to see a real danger in such euphemisms: "if thought corrupts language, language can also corrupt thought. A bad usage can spread by tradition and imitation even among people who should and do know better."[11] In 1940, he was still willing to present a blunt phrase like "necessary murder" as worse than "liquidation" or "euphemism," on the grounds that it betrayed a brazen indifference. Yet notably, the words "necessary murder" are buttressed by the kind of "soothing phrases" that Orwell would later describe so brilliantly in "Politics and the English Language."

Indeed, the preceding line, "the deliberate increase in the chances of death," belongs to the world of euphemism that Orwell attacked in 1940. First, there is the line's grammatical structure: a sequence of prepositional phrases, punting the word "death" further and further down to the end of the line, where its impact can be muted. Second, there is the quality of the speaker's vocabulary. Notice the use of an optimistic "chance" over "risk," for example, and how the risk of death has been abstracted into a numerical matter with "increase." Third, there is the use of an impersonal point of view that obscures responsibility. "Deliberate increase" acknowledges that some people will die and that this will be due to a willful choice, but the nominalization disguises the identity of the person or institution making the decision.

That Orwell had hit on a real problem is clear from Auden's strenuous (if rather weak) self-defense in a letter to Monroe K. Spears dated May 11, 1963: "I was not excusing totalitarian crimes but only trying to say what, surely, every decent person thinks if he finds himself unable to adopt the absolute pacifist position. . . . To kill another human being is always murder and should never be called anything else."[12] The fact that Auden continued to dwell on Orwell's criticisms more than twenty-five years after "Political Reflections on the Crisis" shows how deeply they affected him. Yet it is hard to match his arguments against the poem proper, for the impact of the word "murder" is neutered by the grammatical contortions leading up to it: "the conscious acceptance of guilt in." "Murder" does not break the wash of bureaucratic talk but rather gets subsumed by it, much like "death" in the previous line. The stanza's broader context only reduces its impact further. Consider, for example, how the lines read when set alongside the stanza that comes immediately before:

> To-morrow for the young the poets exploding like bombs,
> The walks by the lake, the weeks of perfect communion;
> To-morrow the bicycle races
> Through the suburbs on summer evenings. But to-day the struggle.[13]

The parallel structure puts everything on a level, both within this stanza and across the poem as a whole, thus erasing any difference in kind among the various and varied items in Auden's list. The glibness of "bicycle races / Through suburbs on summer evenings" sets the tone for the events of the following stanza, so there is little to distinguish the metaphorical violence of inspiration ("To-morrow for the young the poets exploding like bombs") from the literal violence of civil war. The poet treats all of these scenes like fictions, as if their reality had not yet touched him.

Still, Auden is not entirely blind to the dangers to which he falls prey. If Orwell's attack on "Spain" deserve qualification, it is because he fails to acknowledge significant countercurrents in the poem. For example, there is an inkling of doubt in the lines that immediately follow the phrase "necessary murder":

> To-day the expending of powers
> On the flat ephemeral pamphlet and the boring meeting.

The second line evokes the contexts in which "soothing phrases" get produced and dispersed: the bureaucratic meetings of state officials, and the pamphlets released by governments and political groups of all stripes. The word "flat" points to the extreme simplicity and dullness of the language that is to be found there, while "ephemeral" recognizes that their lack of substance also gives them a short shelf life. The fact that the poem first appeared in a pamphlet shows a degree of critical self-awareness that Orwell ignores. Still, there are definite limits to that self-awareness at this juncture in his writing life. While the poem does contain an implicit jab at political rhetoric, "the flat ephemeral pamphlet and the boring meeting" are finally swept up and placed in the category of inconveniences and discomforts that must be endured "to-day" for a better "to-morrow," as the subsequent stanza makes clear:

> To-day the makeshift consolations: the shared cigarette,
> The cards in the candlelit barn, and the scraping concert,
> The masculine jokes; to-day the
> Fumbled and unsatisfactory embrace before hurting.[14]

Here, as well, the parallels reduce distinctions between the political language designed by committee and the "makeshift" entertainments that people must content themselves with during this time. The stanza ends with another euphemistic term for all the violence that comes out of war: "hurting." The fact that this word rhymes with "boring meeting" in the previous stanza has the potential for irony: it is in meetings such as these that future hurts are decided ("the deliberate increase in the chances of death") or encouraged (through the writing of propaganda). But Auden did not wish to activate that potential and so does not emphasize the connection.

"Spain" calls to mind the melancholic definition of propaganda that Auden dreamed up for the 1956 essay "Hic et Ille": "the use of magic by those who no longer believe in it against those who still do."[15] Auden's growing discomfort with "Spain" became evident as early as 1940, when he retitled the poem "Spain 1937" for his book *Another Time,* no doubt in the hope that a date would distance his past self. He would later brand the poem "dishonest" and exclude it entirely from his *Collected Shorter Poems* in 1966.[16] Granted, there are passages in "Spain" that suggest he was already conscious of the problems with his own rhetoric and with the euphemisms deployed in the public sphere. In 1937, however, Auden still believed that the ends mattered more than the means, and so he was willing to downplay these concerns in order to create a politically effective poem. "Spain" marked the end of an era in Auden's writing, as he soon began to develop a more critical approach to the bureaucratic language that he had exploited before.

Auden's reckoning with bureaucratese acquired a new urgency with his move to the United States in January 1939. In America, he found a mass society whose public discourse seemed to him saturated with abstractions. The first poem to come out of his experiences, "The Unknown Citizen" (published in the *Listener* on August 3), takes the form of an elegy for a man whose perfectly average life exposes the uniformity that mass society enforces. The poem is Auden's first significant critique of bureaucratic language, and it achieves these goals through pastiche—by adopting what Bonnie Costello has called "the fickle voice of bureaucracy"[17] and deploying clichés widely. The poem is awash in different types of abstract phrases, all evoking governmental offices ("the Bureau of Statistics," "Producers Research," and "High-Grade Living"), private corporations ("Fudge Motors Inc."), or broader social concepts ("Public Opinion"). Auden's approach at this stage still does not qualify as echo and critique, with its close examination of specific phrases, but it does mark a step in that direction since it shows Auden training a more critical eye on abstractions and commenting on their widespread abuse. Ultimately, his linguistic analysis serves a broader critique of society. Auden's argument is that public and private entities, by treating citizens like data, create a culture of uniformity that brings democracies closer to totalitarianism. It is no coincidence that one of the last figures to appear in the poem is a eugenicist: "[the citizen] was married and added five children to the population, / Which our Eugenist says was the right number for a parent of his generation."[18] This detail evokes the dictatorships of Europe, but it also suggests, as Sinclair Lewis did five years prior, that in fact *it can happen here* in the United States.[19] Indeed, "Fudge Motors, Inc." has a distinctly American ring.

Auden's ideas about mass society during this period were derived from his reading of Søren Kierkegaard. In the essay "Vocation and Society" (1943), Auden contended that, without passion, a democracy "must inevitably dissolve into an amorphous abstraction called the General Public in which everyone is, as Kierkegaard says, 'like the interjection, without influence on the sentence, and at the very most takes a case, e.g., *O me miserum,* and the politicians are like Green reciprocals which are wanting in the nominative singular and all subjective cases, and can only be thought of in the plural and possessive cases.'"[20] Nine years later, Auden edited a volume of the philosopher's writings that included passages expanding on this idea:

> A public is neither a nation, nor a generation, nor a community, nor these particular men, for all these are only what they are though the concrete; no single person who belongs to the public makes a real commitment; for some hours of the day, perhaps, he belongs to the public—at moments when he is nothing else, since when he is really what he is he does not form part of the public. Made up of such individuals, of individuals at the moments when they are nothing, a public is a kind of gigantic something, an abstract and deserted void which is everything and nothing.[21]

The insight of "The Unknown Citizen" was to look beyond the abstract structure of mass society and examine how the abstract language used in that society influences the way that individuals are treated and understood. The poem is not quite written as a governmental report, though that would have been one obvious possibility for satire. Instead, Auden invents a speaker who has total faith in bureaucracy and has absorbed its language and perspective. This is evident in the repeated use of the first-person plural (for example: "our researchers into Public Opinion"), which assumes complete identification with the organisms governing mass society. The speaker might be a state worker, but he might also be just another ordinary citizen. Either way, his view of the world, and the language he uses to talk about the world, has become subsumed by bureaucratese.

The sheer number of abstract phrases in "The Unknown Citizen" leaves Auden little room to examine specific instances in any detail. The poem's satire depends on scale, so that the quality of the phrases is revealed through accumulation rather than close individual attention and analysis. Still, Auden's approach does allow for some broad-strokes commentary. Sound plays a significant role in this regard. Jahan Ramazani has aptly described "the relentless lockstep of mechanical rhymes" in "The Unknown Citizen."[22] The rhymes in the poem's opening passage make a key point:

> He was found by the Bureau of Statistics to be
> One against whom there was no official complaint,

And all the reports on his conduct agree
That, in the modern sense of an old-fashioned word, he was a saint,
For in everything he did he served the Greater Community.[23]

The cloying chime of "agree" with "Greater Community" hints at the uniformity this concept can be used to enforce. The effect is compounded by the capitalization, which grants the phrase a degree of importance that the speaker does not even accord to saints. The effect is sharpened, as well, by its position at the end of a long sentence extending across five lines, so that the phrase appears to bring the report firmly to a close. Even the totalities leading up to it ("no," "all," and "everything") clearly indicate that the "Greater Community" has assumed complete authority over the citizens' lives, or rather that talk of community has been marshaled effectively as a tool for social control. The only note of disagreement in this sentence—the word "complaint"—gets neutered both by the negation that precedes it and the word "saint" that follows it, thereby preventing the rhyme on "complaint" from serving as a true counterpoint to "agree" and "community."

As the poem continues, however, Auden discreetly pushes back against the impersonality of bureaucratic language by using words that introduce human feeling. These words are deeply ironic in that the speaker appears oblivious to their emotional dimension.

Both Producers Research and High-Grade Living declare
He was fully sensible to the advantages of the Instalment Plan

The force of the word "sensible" depends on a double meaning and a paradox. To be sensible is to be reasonable and measured. It implies a reliance on thought rather than emotion, which can be illogical and unstable. But to be sensible *to* something presents a radically different relation between heart and mind. It suggests that a person is sensitive to something, that they are able to approach a given matter by drawing not only on rational thought but also on their own emotions. The two meanings are not quite opposed, but the second does have an additional strand of meaning, one that depicts a far richer way to live. The word here is ironic because the speaker clearly uses it in the first sense, to say that the citizen recognized the advantages of the Instalment Plan because he was so rational. At the same time, the second sense of the word—foregrounded here by the construction "sensible to"—is definitely at play, evoking an emotional life that the citizen certainly had but that bureaucracies could not see. It also, more darkly, reinforces the gap between the citizen's lived experience and the speaker's complete indifference to human feeling, in a poem that is itself devoid of sensibility. Even as the word "sensible" pushes back against this limited view of life, it also finds itself diminished by the capitalized abstractions that crowd around it. There is no doubt that the bureaucratic perspective will always eclipse the individual, as it does at the end of the poem: "Was he free? Was he happy? The question is absurd: / Had anything been wrong, we should certainly have heard."[24]

"The Unknown Citizen" satirizes bureaucratic language through a series of abstract phrases, some of which were common parlance ("Greater Community"), while others were invented for this poem ("Producers Research," "High-Grade Living"). The effects Auden achieves are bold, quick, and not especially subtle. He attacks these phrases for their coercion and their dishonesty, without trying to weigh their implications more closely. But the poem matters to the history of echo and critique; for in Auden's rhymes, and in the contrast that he draws between the word "sensible" and the abstractions that surround it, we find the beginning of a method that he would develop more fully at the start of World War II, with greater attentiveness to the questions that public clichés raise.

For Auden, as for many poets, World War II prompted a reckoning as to the dangers of political rhetoric. The war demonstrated vividly the ways that public discourse can be manipulated to disguise, support, or advance the erosion of democratic freedoms. Auden was living in New York City when the conflict broke out in Europe, with Hitler's invasion of Poland. His poem "September 1, 1939," published in the *New Republic* on October 18, weighs this major historical event against his own individual sensibility. It is a work deeply concerned with public rhetoric, and the ways that rhetoric can be ineffectual or deceptive. He explicitly mentions political speeches ("what dictators do, / The elderly rubbish they talk") and evokes other forms with the image of "the folded lie"—perhaps a reference to newspapers.[25] It is also the first definitive instance of echo and critique in his poetry. For the urgency of this historical moment pushed Auden to bring a far greater degree of scrutiny to the political language of the 1930s and to think about how it might have contributed to a world in which this conflict became possible. In the fourth stanza, he focuses on a phrase that had become common currency in this decade.

> Into this neutral air
> Where blind skyscrapers use
> Their full height to proclaim
> The strength of Collective Man,
> Each language pours its vain
> Competitive excuse[26]

Readers of the poem on its first publication would have immediately recognized "Collective Man," a phrase that was widely used in political discourse throughout the 1930s. Auden puts pressure on the idiom by pitting it against "Competitive excuse" two lines down. (The effect is visually reinforced by the capitalization of "Competitive" thanks to its position at the head of the line.) The pairing asks a provocative question: to what extent is praise of collective action a cover for competitive enterprise? Auden might appear to present these as opposites, so that "Collective Man" stands independently of the "Competitive excuses" that swirl about it. Associating the first phrase with a skyscraper certainly seems to grant it a greater degree of solidity. The contrast between "proclaim" on the one hand, and "vain" and "excuse" on the other, also seems to put more faith in "Collective Man." In this reading, the "vain" excuses of special interest groups are no match for the strength of the collective. But the structure of the sentence casts doubts on that certainty: "Collective Man" finds itself relegated to a subordinate clause, allowing "Competitive excuse" to assert itself more boldly in the main clause. Praise of collective action is now seen as (at best) ineffectual, or (at worst) a conscious distraction from competitive interests. The image of skyscrapers plays into this more pessimistic reading thanks to its association with the business world. Though the buildings may be the result of collective labor, their construction is ordered and funded by business interests, and the offices within certainly serve competitive goals. There is a Marxist idea knocking about the stanza that the skyscraper is built on the labor of a collective body but that it does not serve the collective interests.

This reading of "Collective Man" as a rhetorical cover for competition is all the stronger if one considers the history of the phrase, which was used by a range of different groups throughout the 1930s. These groups included, but were not limited to, Communist leaders in Russia, and the American journalists reporting on those leaders; labor unions on both sides of the Atlantic; as well as philosophers, economists, social scientists, and psychoanalysts.[27] Despite its claims to coherence, "Collective Man" was marshaled toward a variety of ends that were often opposed. Compare, for example, the phrase as it appears in the *Prison Notebooks* of the Italian Marxist philosopher Antonio Gramsci ("Every historical act can only be performed by 'collective man' [*uomo collettivo*]")[28] and the autobiography of the American historian William Henry Chamberlin ("I believe that individual man's instinct is to create, while collective man's instinct is to destroy").[29] The connotation of the phrase was hotly contested, and the competition to control its meaning in public discourse was part of a larger debate around individualism and collectivism: "Each language pours its vain / Competitive excuse." These voices represent, at least in part, the competing claims on "Collective Man," which now seem vain when set against the threat of fascism. The rhetoric of collectivity has become, for Auden, a way to avoid the direct actions required by this historical moment. The skyscrapers also symbolize America's aloofness from world affairs (the United States remaining neutral at this point in the war). As Anthony Hecht has pointed out, "The air is 'neutral' because the poem is set in New York, outside the realm, for the moment, of conflict."[30] In much the same way that "Collective" is revealed to be actually "Competitive," the "neutral" air is exposed as "blind" in the succeeding line. The blindness here is willful and allows the United States to turn away from what Auden felt to be a moral responsibility.

Auden's pairing of "Collective Man" with "Competitive excuse"—the first instance of what I call "echo and critique" in his poetry—is thus richly multivalent, suggesting a number of ways that competitiveness can underlie the rhetoric of collectivity. Yet when Auden tries to develop a more honest account of the political situation, he resorts to abstractions that are akin to what the phrase condemns. This occurs at the end of the stanza when the speaker dismisses the illusions pedaled by "Collective Man."

> Out of the mirror they stare,
> Imperialism's face
> And the international wrong.[31]

For Stephanie Burt, these lines "suggest that we know exactly what or which 'international wrong' Auden means."[32] Certainly, the imagery of the mirror implies that what it reveals is a self-evident truth, demanding to be recognized and accepted; a mirror reflects only what stands before it. Yet what "stares" out of the mirror is not a person, or a place, or an event, but yet another pair of abstractions: "Imperialism's face / And the international wrong." The specific historical referent of "Imperialism" is easy to identify, Nazi Germany having just invaded Poland. But "the international wrong" folds into a single phrase a host of different possible faults—not only German aggression but the passivity of the United States and western Europe—that are distinct situations but bundled ambiguously into one. The boldness of Auden's phrase conceals the vagueness of what it condemns. "The international wrong" not only simplifies; it evades by refusing to name the culprit, or rather culprits, and thus declining to make finer distinctions between the players in this historical tragedy.

Auden's slip reveals the difficulty of talking about public affairs without falling into empty or evasive abstractions, even when one is conscious of the problem in others. Randall Jarrell knew this and wrote, in his essay on Auden, about the need for constant vigilance: "Stylistic rectitude, like any other, is something that has to be worked at all the time, a struggle—like sleeping or eating or living—that permits only temporary victories; and nothing us makes us more susceptible to a vice than the knowledge that we have already overcome it."[33] Auden became aware of this necessity, too. A couple of months after the publication of "September 1, 1939," he started work on a poem where he conceded his susceptibility to the political clichés he wished to push back against.

From January to April 1940, Auden devoted his attention to a long poem titled "New Year Letter." In it, Auden attempts to take stock of the social, political, and moral issues of the present. The poem has been criticized for what Michael Murphy terms its neoclassical form: the octosyllabic couplet.[34] To Edward Mendelson's ear, "the conservative order of its syntax and metre struggled to restrain the anarchic whirlwind of its ideas."[35] Still, that "anarchic whirlwind" also serves a particular purpose, offering a necessary counterpoint to the uniformity of public discourse. This is an idea that we have seen in Auden before. Here, though, he confronts not only the clichés peddled in political speech but also his own involvement in the dissemination of cliché: a significant turn in Auden's thinking about rhetoric. The first stanza establishes this concern in its description of a busy street scene. The opening sentence ends climactically with three terms central to public discourse.

> Under the familiar weight
> Of winter, conscience and the State,
> In loose formations of good cheer,
> Love, language, loneliness and fear,
> Towards the habits of next year,
> Along the streets the people flow,
> Singing or sighing as they go:
> *Exalté, piano,* or in doubt,
> All our reflections turn about
> A common meditative norm,
> Retrenchment, Sacrifice, Reform.[36]

For Auden, the words "retrenchment," "sacrifice," and "reform" so dominate political rhetoric that they have been emptied of meaning. Yet a reflexive use does not mean they have no impact. On the contrary, their dominance further restricts the ideas expressed in the public sphere by crowding out alternatives. "Retrenchment," "sacrifice," and "reform" are now the expected thing, and no political figure can do without them. This argument is communicated two ways. First, in the penultimate line, with the word "common" hardening into "norm": a consensus devolving into a set of rules and restrictions. Second, by the progression of the stanza as a whole. Auden begins by working through a series of lists, all marked by their variety: "winter, conscience, and the State"; "loose formations" of moods and emotions; diverse styles of song and speech in "*Exalté, piano,* or in doubt." Variety makes the uniformity of public rhetoric all the more striking. The last line presents a false plurality that is in fact a "norm." This sameness is reflected, in turn, by the depiction of movement. The people may "flow . . . along the streets," but their reflections merely "turn about" in a circuitous motion, going nowhere.

Auden's evaluation of these key words may appear counterintuitive, since the terms usually reflect different political sensibilities. If "retrenchment" can stand comfortably alongside "sacrifice," as both reflect a conservative response to crisis akin to "belt-tightening" and "cost-cutting" (to name two other clichés), "reform" suggests a more radical outlook, based on structural change rather than a reduction of cost. But the rhyme on "norm" neuters that distinction, so that "reform" gets folded into the blank hum of political discourse. Even talk of change has become par for the course. The capitalization pushes this argument further by suggesting that the terms cannot be understood as a reflection of genuine political commitments. "Reform" no longer truly means "reform" because the word has become an empty gesture, evoking a popular attitude rather than declaring a concrete agenda. Together, "Retrenchment," "Sacrifice," and "Reform" have the narrowness of slogans: they are short and memorable phrases, deployed repetitively to indicate (and encourage) allegiance, whose function has thinned to a single possibility.

In "New Year Letter," we find another example of a method that Auden developed fully in "September 1, 1939." But the poem also marks another important step forward. Prior to "New Year Letter," Auden tended to blame the corruption of political rhetoric on abstract entities distinct from the poet and the public. The clichés in "The Unknown Citizen" stem from bureaucracies that are invisible yet everywhere present. Similarly, the phrase "Collective Man" is associated with looming skyscrapers that represent, in Peter Edgerly Firchow's terms, "that larger, more abstract and anti-spiritual social machine."[37] In "New Year Letter," however, clichés are placed firmly in the minds (and mouths) of ordinary citizens, and these include the poet: "All *our* reflections turn about / A common meditative norm." Rhetorical corruption cannot simply be attributed to the institutions that create or peddle clichés; the ordinary citizens who then repeat and make use of those phrases in turn become complicit. This marks a departure from Auden's previous work, signaling a new awareness of his responsibilities with regard to public discourse, both as a poet and as a citizen.

The period between "Spain" and "New Year Letter" witnessed a fundamental shift in Auden's attitude toward political language and political clichés, from a conscious participant in the rhetoric of his time, to a critical—if necessarily imperfect—examiner. This evolution became part of a broader shift in the way he understood poetry's function. As Humphrey Carpenter has shown, Auden came to believe that, "though he is to avoid direct involvement in social issues, the artist is nevertheless called upon to 'set in order,' to organize our perceptions of the world."[38] In "New Year Letter," Auden concedes that "language may be useless, for / No words men write can stop the war / Or measure up to the relief / Of its immeasurable grief," but that poetry can and should still serve as an "*aide-mémoire*" where "heart and intelligence" assert themselves.[39] He had previously introduced this idea in his elegy for W. B. Yeats (dated February 1939), where he wrote that while "poetry makes nothing happen," it "survives / In the valley of its making" as "a way of happening, a mouth."[40] This was followed by an essay, "The Public v. the Late Mr. William Butler Yeats," published in the spring 1939 issue of the *Partisan Review,* where he claimed that art "does not re-enter history as an effective agent"; that "if not a poem had been written, nor a picture painted, not a bar of music composed, the history of man would be materially unchanged"; but that despite all this, "there is one field in which the poet is a man of action, the field of language."[41] To Auden, what the poet can do is use language responsibly, hold public rhetoric accountable, and exert counterpressure on the way that words are deployed in the political sphere—even if poets, like all other citizens, cannot assume they will not fall prey to the same ills that are everywhere present in political discourse.

Ironically, these ideas are consonant with Orwell's essay "Inside the Whale." While it is here that he expanded his attacks on Auden, he also believed that a writer can have only a limited impact in the realm of political action (although, unlike Auden, he attributed this to the historical situation rather than the nature of literary writing itself):

While I have been writing this essay another European war has broken out. It will either last several years and tear Western civilization to pieces, or it will end inconclusively and prepare the way for yet another war which will do the job once and for all. . . . But from now onwards the all-important fact for the creative writers going to be that this is not a writer's world. That does not mean that he cannot help to bring the new society into being, but he can take no part in the process as a writer. For as a writer he is a liberal, and what is happening is the destruction of liberalism.

Despite these challenges, Orwell argues that the writer still has an important role to play as a critical observer and commentator. He offers the following advice: "Give yourself over to the world-process, stop fighting against it or pretending that you control it; simply accept it, endure it, record it. That seems to be the formula, that any sensitive novelist is now likely to adopt." Or any poet. Auden's complex, self-reflective use of echo and critique became a touchstone for other poets of the postwar era who wanted to confront public clichés without losing sight of their own susceptibility to the mechanisms of evasive political language. His influence would extend far beyond the immediate circle of what has been called the Auden Group, who shared other features of his style, to poets of different aesthetic sensibilities, and even writers like Randall Jarrell who openly criticized him. Yet this, too, is a testament to the compelling force of this method as it continued to develop in the decades following the start of World War II.

2

RANDALL JARRELL

ON

WAR PROPAGANDA

AND THE

AMERICAN SOLDIER

Randall Jarrell criticized Auden for his overreliance on abstract stock phrases, but it was in reading Auden that he found a technique to apprehend those abstractions in his own writing. For Jarrell, as for many others, the Second World War lent special urgency to the problem of corruption in political language, both in dictatorships like Germany and in democracies like the United States. Nazi propaganda provided chilling examples of stock phrases created to lie, manipulate, and conceal atrocities. Yet even as Jarrell recognized the need to gather support in the fight against fascism, he detected in the propagandist speeches, posters, radio, and film shorts of the United States the same linguistic tricks—like abstraction or euphemism—used by totalitarian regimes in Europe. Echo and critique allowed him to examine the stock phrases of American war propaganda without simply dismissing them.

It should be noted that Jarrell was not the only poet to confront American war propaganda in his verse. If Auden provided a model for how a poet might apply echo and critique to the clichés of public discourse, World War II was the historical turning point that prompted other writers to adopt this method in turn. The rhetorical parallels between democracy and dictatorship made it all the more essential to scrutinize the phrases of war propaganda in the United States, and in doing so to hold American political rhetoric accountable. This is a feature of World War II poetry that has received little attention. Indeed, while several critics—such as Melissa Dinsman, Matthew Feldman, and Susan Schweik—have either considered the propaganda that American writers contributed, or analyzed individual poems for their propagandist function, little has been said about how poets echoed particular instances of propagandist language in their work, holding them up for scrutiny, drawing out their implications, and examining their effects.[1]

Poets did this work amid a tense public debate around propaganda, which was alternately viewed as a necessary tool in the fight against fascism or as a dangerous sign of corruption in public discourse. With the decision to enter the war in 1941, Roosevelt sought to reassure Americans that his administration would not enact broad government censorship.[2] Still, the opening of the Office of War Information the following year stirred controversy among journalists, congressional members, and the US military, who were concerned about the creation of a government agency charged with propagandist communication.[3] At the same time, the war also prompted numerous defenses of mass persuasion. Eduard Lindeman and Clyde Miller's introduction to *War Propaganda and the United States,* published a year before American intervention in 1940, opens with the words: "We live in a propaganda age. Public opinion no longer is formulated by the slow processes of what Professor John Dewey calls shared experience. In our time public opinion is primarily a response to propaganda stimuli." But then the authors immediately qualify:

Whether or not the above statements are regarded as true depends upon one's definition of propaganda. If, for example, one condemns all propaganda as being vicious, then the above statements cannot possibly be true. On the other hand, if one assumes that propaganda is a method utilized for influencing the conduct of others on behalf predetermined ends, it appears that every articulate person with a purpose is a propagandist. From this viewpoint it would hence be more fair to state that ours is an age of competing propagandas.[4]

To Lindeman and Miller, the term cannot be limited to material deemed "vicious": even propaganda against Nazism, for example, should still be called so as well. By the end of the paragraph, however, Lindeman and Miller have broadened the word's reach to the point of including most anyone "with a purpose"; likely, a purpose to convince others, but the wording casts an even wider net: "From this viewpoint it would hence be fairer to state that ours is an age of competing propagandas." The authors make propaganda obscurely synonymous with opinion and equate any attempt to convince an audience of a given idea with the mass persuasion of governments. The simplification is extreme, but it allows the authors to make state propaganda appear less threatening (the state is just one voice among others) and to frame propaganda itself as entirely compatible with democracy rather than as a potential threat to it.

As this debate continued, poets took different approaches to the stock phrases of Allied propaganda. I would like to consider two examples here so as to bring out the distinctiveness of Jarrell's approach by contrast. It is important to note, first, that not all poets critiqued the phrases they echoed. Some aimed instead to reinforce them or provide them with another platform and thus contribute to "the war effort" (itself a cliché). One notable instance is Marianne Moore's "Walking-Stick and Paperweights and Watermarks" (1941), a poem that is all the more surprising if one considers the skeptical eye that its author brings to other subjects.

> "Airmail is quick." "Save rags, bones, metals."
>   Hopes
> are harvest when deeds follow
>   words postmarked "Dig for victory."[5]

In this passage, Moore slips quickly from advertising ("Airmail is quick") to propaganda ("Save rags, bones, metals," "Dig for victory"). The difference between these two types of public communication is a complex problem, yet the seamless transition silences this issue altogether. Since advertising is, by and large, not viewed as critically as propaganda, the pairing serves to make propaganda appear harmless by association. But Moore does more than simply diminish the doubts that her readers may have about this discourse. She also buttresses the slogan "Dig for victory" by expanding its central metaphor. The phrase was key to campaigns in Allied countries urging citizens to plant their own fruits, vegetables, and herbs to supplement their rations.[6] This slogan appeared not only in the usual media for propaganda (posters, radio, and short films) but also as postmarks. Moore fulfills the metaphorical possibilities of the phrase: from digging there comes a "harvest," one made up of "hopes." For the crop to succeed, however, it is essential that words give way to actions. "Hopes / are harvest *when* deeds follow / words." Moore does not mean that hope can only be achieved by setting up a victory garden, but she does argue that this is one of the deeds that should be put into action. Far from the spirit of echo and critique, which is founded on skepticism, Moore echoes a phrase in order to lend her support. Indeed, the poem succumbs to propaganda in turn by spurring her readers to action.

At the other end of the spectrum, some poets during the war took a baldly satirical approach to the stock phrases of military propaganda by ridiculing their pretenses and pretentiousness. Ogden Nash's play on the concept of a "Victory Garden" in 1943 offers a striking contrast to Moore. Nash takes the association of gardening and war already present in the phrase "Victory Garden" and sets it in the world of medieval knights by way of mockery. This context exposes the silliness of coupling international combat and domestic agriculture: gardening, after all, can only seem petty and minor when compared to the pain of real warfare. After addressing his readers formally as though he were beginning a speech ("Today, my friends, I beg your pardon, / But I'd like to speak of my Victory Garden"), the speaker compares his gardening materials to weaponry and armor. He carries "a hoe for a sword, and citronella for armor," both parallels serving to ridicule rather than elevate. Other deflating touches include the description of him "perspiring *clammily*" (an adverb denoting fragility, not often associated with knights in shining armor), as well as repeated drops in linguistic register through awkward phrasing ("A figure than which there was none more dramatic-er," itself overly dramatic with the double comparative) and clunky, informal rhymes ("I toiled with the patience of Job or Buddha, / But nothing turned out the way it shudda").[7] The result is quixotic, in the sense that Nash pokes fun at misplaced ambition.

While Jarrell was highly critical of propagandist clichés, he was careful not to simply dismiss them, for he recognized how easily the term "propaganda" can be brandished to avoid confronting alternative points of view. In a letter to Amy Breyer de Blasio written while he was in the US Air Force, he disparaged his fellow soldiers on these very grounds:

> They feel neither gratitude nor affection for our allies—they'd fight Russia tomorrow, for instance. They have no feeling against the Germans—they dismiss all information about them as "propaganda." This *propaganda* is their one response, frightening and invariable, to anything they haven't always known (and they have known almost nothing). The innocent idealism and naïve whipped-up hatred (which collapsed into fraternizing when it really encountered the enemy in the first World War) were a good deal better than this.[8]

For Jarrell, "propaganda" has become a verbal tag by which new or divergent ideas can be speedily rejected: in other words, my opinions are founded on a reasoned view of the world, whereas yours are the result of public manipulation. Jarrell goes on to favor the "innocent idealism and naïve whipped-up hatred" of World War I: the work of military propaganda on both sides of the ocean. Such illusions are deemed less permanently seductive—and so less dangerous—than apathy, which can color one's whole perspective. But Jarrell must have realized that there was something a little too tidy about the claim that idealism and hatred "collapsed into fraternizing when it really encountered the enemy in the first World War." The parentheses do not help and give the impression he is padding his statements to make history fit his dismissal of present-day attitudes.

His evasiveness suggests a creeping awareness that in trying to counter an overly lax use of the term "propaganda," he risked defending the thing itself.

For Jarrell, real propaganda—the promotion of political ideas by distorting or selectively deploying information—abuses its audience by demanding that it submit uncritically to a cause, no matter how right and necessary. Jarrell felt this to be a significant danger in the United States during World War II: a time when "the cause" was undeniably right, and when institutional changes had facilitated the spread and effectiveness of military propaganda. As Lorrie Goldensohn has shown, Jarrell believed that the war had led to the fusion of the army and the State into a vast, intangible, and totalitarian entity.[9] We see this in "The State," a poem that adopts a child's perspective to better understand the psychology of submitting oneself to an omnipotent governing body. In scrambling to forgive the State for killing their mother, the speaker reaches for a cluster of bizarre explanations: "Of course she was crazy, and how she ate! / And she died, after all, in her way, for the State."[10] As she nervously winds her way through excuses, her syntax is broken up by pauses and modulations ("she died, after all, in her way"). She finally arrives at a common phrase ("to die for your country") only to find that the idea of nationhood has been supplanted by an impersonal State. And with the morbid click of a rhyme on "ate," the State reaches up and gobbles up mother.

Jarrell made use of a similar image in a letter to his wife, Mackie Langham, during the war: "Being in the army is like being involved in the digestive process of an immense worm or slug or something—being involved in them along with tens of thousands around you and millions out of your sight; it doesn't seem terribly stupid or at all malicious, just too big to have any sense or meaning—a mess rather."[11] For Jarrell, the most pernicious effect of inhabiting such a system is that it robs individuals of individuality and turns them into data. The poem "Eighth Air Force" cannily illustrates this by playing on the word "one": "Three of them play Pitch, one sleeps, and one / Lies counting missions . . . Till even his heart beats: One; One; One."[12] War is a numbers game ("counting missions"), and the soldiers become numbers in turn: "three," "one," "one." A soldier is identified with his heartbeat ("One; One; One"), but the capitalization of that final sequence does little to counteract his anonymity. The heartbeats become themselves monotonous, in the same way that the shock of the word "murderers" is utterly blunted by its context.

The complexities of Jarrell's views on propaganda are evident in his echoes of propagandist language, in particular phrases that center on moral abstractions like "truth," "freedom," "honor," "glory," "courage," "good," and "evil." To him, such phrases carry tremendous power because the ideas they represent are indeed valuable, or rather can be valuable in particular manifestations. To say freedom does not exist or cannot exist is to endorse a brand of moral relativism that Jarrell viewed with profound suspicion, as an escape from personal and public responsibility. Yet these abstractions were routinely exploited in ways that went against, or fell short of, the ideals they were meant to promote. His aim was to test these words against specific instances and to emphasize the importance of particulars in the face of propaganda's insistence on the general.

At the same time, Jarrell's attempts to distance himself from propaganda was complicated by war poetry's reliance on abstraction. After all, to describe the experience of war through the use of a representative figure is to traffic in a kind of abstraction: the Soldier, whose thoughts and feelings express those of all soldiers everywhere. This was especially a risk in World War II poetry, due to both the technology deployed in battle and the specific background of the poets who fought in the war. As Diederik Oostdijk points out:

> Most of the World War II poets were not in the infantry, so they did not encounter similar events that Owen, Rosenberg, and Sassoon had penned about the First World War. Many of the American poets of World War II were instead in the air corps. Not only does this fact reflect an innovation in warfare, it also means that these war poets offered, literally and figuratively, a different perspective of war. From high above, they could see what a puny creature a human being is, and how helpless they themselves were, trapped in their war machines.[13]

And indeed, several critics have accused Jarrell of succumbing to the very habits he strove to resist. W. S. Graham, in a review of his 1948 collection *Losses,* conceded just this:

Because most of the poems . . . deal with a war environment one ex-
pects them to contain the antithesis of life and death (that is, both
as subjects objectified by the created poem, as well as common
subject, by implication, in all poems), yet here they are embossed
and studded with capitalized Life's and Deaths throughout. . . . I
had supposed the snare of the old abstract poetic gear would be
more cunningly handled by a poet of Mr. Jarrell's training. Here he
allows the poem to dissolve into "vague immensities."[14]

James Dickey adopted a similar line of attack: "I don't think there are really any people in the war poems. There are only The Ball Turret Gunner,
A Pilot from the Carrier, The Wingman, and assorted faceless types in
uniform. They are just collective Objects, or Attitudes, or Killable Puppets. You care very little what happens to them, and that is terrible."[15] One
might choose to defend Jarrell, as Paul Fussell has, by claiming that the ob-
jectification is very much to the point: the army treats its combatants like
killable puppets, and Jarrell's poems reproduce that attitude to confront us
with its effects.[16] But this does not quite exonerate Jarrell from the charge
that he bought into abstractions instead of pushing against them. Suzanne
Ferguson argues as much when she says that his poems reveal "a tendency
to pity individuals for their sufferings and deaths while blaming such abstractions as Trade or the States for the apparently insatiable impulse to
aggrandizement that seemed to Jarrell the source of all men's misery."[17]
To think of the world in terms of Trade and States is to align oneself with
the powers that want to be thought of as such, giving the words too much
credence. Yet Jarrell was conscious of this risk both in others and in himself. His essay "Changes of Attitude and Rhetoric in Auden's Poetry" is
proof of that. In the winter 1945 issue of the *Paris Review*, Jarrell similarly
criticized Marianne Moore's "In Distrust of Merits" for treating war, and
the soldiers fighting in the war, as abstractions: "She does not understand
that they are heroes in the sense that the chimney sweeps, the factory children in the blue books, were heroes: routine loss in the routine business
of the world. She sees them (the recurring triplet is the major theme of
the poem) *fighting fighting fighting;* she does not remember that most of
the people in a war never fight for even a minute—though they bear and
die forever."[18] By not staying true to the experience of life in the army,

Moore had abstracted her soldiers and identified them solely with their official function. Regardless of whether his essays on Auden and Moore made fair criticisms of either poet, these lines reveal the extent of Jarrell's preoccupations. For him, the abstractions deployed in propaganda posed a very real danger to poetry as well. In his own poems, Jarrell would seek to curtail these risks, even as his conflicted sense of abstractions as half-lies and half-truths—words that we should both resist and value—gave him a more nuanced view of propaganda than was commonly held in the debates that animated the 1940s.

Jarrell's war poetry is notable for the complicated feelings it expresses about propaganda, at a time when much of the public debate had fallen to extremes. Yet I would like to briefly consider a poem where Jarrell adopts a purely oppositional stance in order to cover his main objections to the clichés that populated this type of mass rhetoric. Here is the first stanza of "A Lullaby":

> For wars his life and half a world away
> The soldier sells his family and days
> He learns to fight for freedom and the State;
> He sleeps with seven men within six feet.[19]

Jarrell contrasts a common propagandist phrase—"fight for freedom," a slogan drawn on posters across the nation during the war—with the reality that supposedly underpins it. Here the call to fight yields not, a line later, to expansive liberty but to the cramped quarters of an army barracks. We land on the measurement of "six feet" at the end of the line only to grasp, with a jolt, its proximity to the phrase "six feet under," suggesting that the soldiers are either sleeping side by side or are buried side by side in a mass grave. The poem asks readers, quite boldly, to note a contrast between the abstract values touted in propaganda and the real-life experience that goes on behind them and in their name. Under the guise of freedom, soldiers are asked to give up theirs and perhaps even to lose their lives: the very possibility of freedom.

Jarrell contrasts two types of abstraction the soldier has been taught to defend: "freedom" and "the State," the abstract value and the abstracted institution that exploits terms of this kind. The line plays out as an act of disillusionment and redress: the lie of "freedom" debunked by "the State" that supplants it. You, the soldier, think you are fighting for the first, but you are actually fighting for the second, and abstract values are merely a cover for the survival of a government bureaucracy. The previous line takes this pessimism further. "The soldier sells his family and days" is a cynical take on the patriotic phrase "paying a debt to one's country" (another cliché). In its original form, the saying makes a moral claim about what citizens owe their country and uses money to illustrate a principle through metaphor. In rewriting the phrase, Jarrell simplifies and underlines the economic language to show that the metaphor was always more literal than its patriotic usage admits. War is a business that requires a grim transaction of its soldiers: family and days, without receiving anything in return. This second line connects back to the first and rewrites "For" in "For wars his life" to mean both "his life in service of war" and "his life in exchange of war." It also sets up a similar transaction in the succeeding line with "fight for freedom and the State."

The objections "A Lullaby" raises about propaganda are simple ones, and indeed they risk being too simple. The poem proceeds largely by direct contrast and demystification. Jarrell, however, must have realized that he could go only so far by debunking what he considered to be untruths. To his credit, his other war poems offer a far more nuanced reading of propagandist language—one in which we are asked to consider the possible value of abstract words; whether abstractions are to be rejected on principle or for the specific ways in which propaganda uses them; and what we stand to lose by doing away with "honor," "freedom," and "truth" altogether. The first stanza of "Port of Embarkation" turns on just these questions:

Freedom, farewell! Or so the soldiers say;
And all the freedoms they spent yesterday
Lure from beyond the graves, a war away.
The cropped skulls resonate the wistful lies

Of dead civilians: truth, reason, justice;
The foolish ages haunt their unaccepting eyes.[20]

At first glance, the poem might appear to fall into the same kinds of oppositions that dominated "A Lullaby." "Truth, reason, justice" are defined one line prior as "wistful lies," so that Jarrell disabuses us of abstract morals before we even arrive at an example. By contrasting the plural form of "lies" with the singular forms of "truth, reason, justice," he suggests that value words are deceitful because of their monolithic singularity. Propaganda makes a claim for truth, reason, and justice, when there are actually truths, reasons, and justices. The fact that "justice" breaks the pattern of full rhymes with an off rhyme only adds to the dissonance between the soldiers' lived reality as they prepare themselves for war, and the language used to spur them on.

Yet there are ambiguities here that enable Jarrell to do far more than oppose the abstractions of propaganda. "The cropped skulls resonate the wistful lies / Of dead civilians: truth, reason, justice." Are these abstractions in fact "wistful lies," or are they "dead civilians"? The isolation of "dead civilians" in the second line and the use of a colon certainly make this latter reading possible, though it might initially seem improbable. If we follow the logic of this through, the poem could be said to envision moral values as personified allegories of civil virtues. They are "dead" because the world has ceased to value them. Jarrell believes truth, reason, and justice are worthy of respect, and what the poem actually objects to is the fact of their being used so cheaply. The civilian reading is supported by the fact that other lines in the poem find great importance in abstract values. Consider the play on singular and plural in the first three lines: "Freedom, farewell! Or so the soldiers say; / And all the freedoms they spent yesterday / Lure from beyond the graves, a war away." The shift from singular to plural indicates a tragic scattering of freedom into all the individual expressions that the soldier must give up. For the pain of this to come home, however, the reader must be willing to take the abstract idea of freedom in earnest. In other words, it is essential to the poem that we understand the soldiers are in fact bidding liberty farewell when they go off to war. To deny the existence of such values would be to deny the very real freedoms that soldiers must surrender when they join the army.

Similarly, to deny the existence of truth, reason, and justice because they have been turned into lies would be to forget what a society stands to lose by abandoning such ideals. Far from debunking the abstract values of propaganda, Jarrell encourages us to think about them more seriously.

This, of course, leads to the question of how to tell when abstractions are being properly or improperly used. Jarrell deems "truth, reason, justice" to be lies when they are trotted out for their pleasing connotations rather than for their meaning, with little regard to what such ideals might require of those who wish to uphold them. Jarrell emphasizes this by arranging the three terms into a casual, and all too interchangeable, sequence. "Truth, reason, justice" could be rewritten as "justice, truth, reason"—the line as it stands does not rhyme anyway—and for that matter any of the three words just mentioned could be replaced by "honor" or "courage." The 1944 film short *A Challenge to Democracy* had relied on a comparable sequence in its final narration: "They know what they're fighting against, and they know what they're fighting for: their country and for the American ideals that are part of their upbringing: democracy, freedom, equality of opportunity regardless of race, creed, or ancestry."[21] To Jarrell, truth, reason, and justice have foundered because they are no longer tethered to concrete particulars. Instead, they serve primarily to create immediate effects and tremors. Even as this poem asks us to weigh what we stand to lose by rejecting the ideals these words represent, it also encourages us to test the words against particular instances, where they may be evaluated more critically.

To Jarrell, war propaganda is most effective and dangerous when it plays into an audience's vulnerabilities, either by describing an ideal they feel pressured to emulate or by appeasing profound anxieties of abandonment carried over from childhood. As Helen Vendler once put it: "The secret of his war poems is that in the soldiers he found children; what is the ball turret gunner but a baby who has lost his mother?"[22] Or, to quote from Richard Fein:

> To the persons of Jarrell's world, experience is like a dream; the
> world is a place where they are lost like frightened children. It
> is the theme of entrapment, this perennial and wistful sense of

unfulfillment, of being lost, which dominates the character of his poetry. The detachment of the individual experience of war from the public slogans and the isolation of the private suffering from what the state demands and history acknowledges produce for the persons of Jarrell's poetry an unrelenting and usually helpless exposure to the realities of war and enforce the awareness that the ragged activities of war are knitted to the soiled fabric of overall experience.[23]

The soldiers in his poems all fear that someone might discover how their worries of abandonment, their longing for comfort, their creeping suspicion that they might not truly be needed by anyone, all impinge upon their adult lives, where they are expected to be strong. Jarrell saw the public slogans of propaganda as attempting to manipulate their audience by preying on these very fears.

For example, his long poem "Siegfried" (the title alludes to Wagner's opera about a tragic war hero) focuses in on the propagandist claim that each individual citizen is "wanted," "needed," "essential," or "indispensable" to the war effort, and so must enlist. This rhetoric became commonplace in England during World War I, where a 1914 poster showing the Secretary of War Lord Kitchener with his finger pointed at the viewer—the words "WANTS YOU" in bold, black lettering underneath his picture—spawned a number of imitations, most famously Uncle Sam's "I Want You for U.S. Army" two years later. With the advent of World War II, this language was adopted for a number of recruitment posters, with slogans like "Become a Nurse: Your Country Needs You" and "The Bugle Sounds: Enlist in the U.S. Army Now. Your Country Needs You." The 1941 short *Women in Defense,* narrated by Katherine Hepburn, offers a parallel example in film: "Again we turn to the women who are asking, 'What can I do for defense?' The American Women's Voluntary Services provides instruction in many basic skills to over 80,000 women. Soon the office of civilian defense will cooperate, not only with AWVS, but with all other private and public agencies, to aid voluntaries in obtaining the training they want: a training indispensable in war, valuable in peace."[24]

"Siegfried," a poem dealing with the incomprehension of soldiers faced with events beyond their control, turns to this rhetoric after describing the machinery of modern warfare (the ball turret, "the bomb's lost patterning"):

It happens as it does because it does.
It is unnecessary to understand; if you are still
In this year of our warfare, indispensable
In general, and in particular dispensable
As a cartridge, a life—[25]

The lulling reassurance—*"It happens as it does because it does"*—is to be
read as a sad evocation of the comforts offered on posters and film shorts,
telling the audience that they are "indispensable" after all. Not that Jarrell
discounts such language altogether. Indeed, the poem does not deny that
the soldiers are "indispensable" but rather qualifies the extent to which
they can be so in the eyes of the army. The distinction Jarrell draws goes
something like this: the army deems soldiers "indispensable / In general"
because the army always needs soldiers to fill its ranks and carry on the
work of war; "in particular," however, soldiers are all too "dispensable"
because any individual soldier can be replaced by another to perform the
same job. Propaganda tries to persuade each person of his indispensability
to the war effort; Jarrell pushes back by saying that the individual is less
important than his function, and in fact every soldier must be replaceable,
and so dispensable, for the army to keep perpetuating itself. The poem
brings the tragedy of this home by yoking "a cartridge, a life" together in
a comparative clause. The soldier is aligned with an object that represents
his function in the army (expendable ammunition) and that will no doubt
bring his own life to an end. "Cartridge" thereby ricochets forward and
back across a line, underlining the self-destructiveness of the task the soldier has entered into, even as the placing of "life" in a comparative clause
serves as a reminder that the army cannot afford to think of individual
soldiers as having or being a life, only of being like a life.

The most important point Jarrell makes in this poem, though, comes
through in a linguistic paradox. By pitting "indispensable" against its
grammatical opposite "dispensable," Jarrell argues that the opposite of
being deemed essential lies not in being hated or despised (as one might
expect), but in being all too easy to do away with. What makes the army
so difficult to endure is that no individual can count for much—not out
of any malice on the army's part but because this is what warfare itself
demands. *"It happens as it does because it does."* Benjamin Friedlander was

right, then, when he said that "Siegfried" "is less about air battles and disfiguring violence, or even about guilt, than it is about the crisis of subjectivity that the war in its technological manifestation poses to its human agents."[26] That crisis of subjectivity is brought about, at least in part, by the realization that the comforts of propaganda simply will not, and cannot, translate to the day-to-day experience of war. The crux of the problem, Jarrell suggests, is that propaganda plays into hopes and expectations that reality will never be able to satisfy.

Jarrell's understanding of the modern army-state as a vast and impersonal institution made him sensitive to propaganda's manifestations beyond the forms typically associated with it (like the poster or the film short). One example would be the communiqués sent by army headquarters to the media relating the outcome of a battle or the progress of a given contingent. Though the ostensible purpose of such messages was to inform and not to persuade, Jarrell believed they had taken on a rhetorical function and served as propaganda for the US Army, eliciting support from the public.

Communiqués are especially difficult to take apart because they do not rely on the usual linguistic schemes of abstraction. Instead, one usually finds the formal properties of journalism: clarity, plain style, apparent objectivity of tone and perspective. Surprisingly, Jarrell argued that these characteristics were used in the service of obfuscation, to soften or conceal aspects of an event that might have an undesirable effect on the audience. The poem "Losses," in which a soldier describes the sad absurdities of military life, echoes this sort of language as it nears an end: "When we lasted long enough they gave us medals; / When we died they said, 'Our casualties were low.'"[27] The quote was a standard phrase in army communiqués, as the next few examples will show. January 17, 1943: "During the evening, enemy planes bombed United States positions on Guadalcanal Island. Minor material damage was inflicted and some casualties among our troops were suffered."[28] March 18, 1943: "During the night of March 15–16, light naval surface forces bombarded Japanese positions at Vila on the southeast coast of Kolombangara Island. Good results were reported and no casualties were suffered by our forces."[29] November 2, 1944: "Our medium and light bombers dropped forty-five tons on enemy airdromes and defenses with good effect. Air patrols destroyed three barges and a coastal craft. We lost one fighter. Seven enemy planes raided our Morotai positions before dawn, causing only minor casualties."[30]

In his poem, Jarrell suggests that the communiqué obscures, first, by reduction. The soldier's experience, in all its nuances and strangeness of detail, gets reduced to an evaluation: how bad was it on the whole? Not that bad, as "our casualties were low." The range of verbs used by the soldier to describe their experience in the previous lines ("we read," "we burned," "we wore," "we lay") gives way to the plainness of the copula "is." Jarrell also calls attention to the use of specialized vocabulary in this genre. While the title "Losses" evokes the language of mourning, "casualties" implies that the soldiers' deaths were the unlucky consequence of something that could not be helped. To Jarrell, the army communiqué is manipulative in that it tries to convince audiences to think positively about the war, even when the war incurs losses (as it often does), while at the same time claiming to provide an objective account of the conflict's progress.

There is some question of how far Jarrell's accusations go. For a poem intent on exposing the army's hypocritical treatment of soldiers (again with a contrast: "When we lasted long enough they gave us medals; / When we died they said, 'Our casualties were low'"), the tone remains even-keeled throughout. Nor does it seem quite right to call this a poem of protest, in the same way that Wilfred Owen's "Dulce et Decorum Est" or later Denise Levertov's Vietnam War poems are works of protest. Stephanie Burt was responding to a similar problem when she wrote:

> Most of [Jarrell's] poems cannot be called pacifist—but neither can it be said that they accept the war's "Losses" as necessary, or justified. Instead, their deliberately unstable tones incorporate both the perspective, the *longue durée,* from which the lost lives must, objectively, be sacrificed and the minute-by-minute perspective according to which each life is everything.... Either we see things from his point of view or we do not; either we credit his extinguished person with infinite value or we tally his corpse along with others—saying perhaps, as the (adult) authorities in "Losses" say, "the casualties were low."[31]

Burt's "either-or" formulation is worth amending, since it implies that "Losses" gives us these points of view as alternatives to choose from, when in fact the particular crisis of subjectivity in this poem stems from the validity of both perspectives. To the soldier, each individual life is important and so cannot be reduced; the army, however, can deal only in relative numbers. Jarrell never insinuates that the army ought somehow to deal with each soldier in all his individual complexity; indeed, he seems patently aware that it would be impossible for the army to do so. Rather the poem laments a clash of perspectives that cannot, and will never be, reconciled. If Jarrell's sympathies lie with the soldiers, it is because he sensed that lyric poetry could voice the point of view of the individual, whereas the army expresses its own through mass media.

"Losses" also reveals Jarrell's own uncertainties as to how he might truthfully depict the war in verse, so that his attacks against the army can go only so far. The title alone is provocative, since it would be easy to accuse the term "losses" of being evasive. As a nominalization, the word makes an object out of an action, obscures those who are lost or have caused the losses to happen, and puts the emphasis on processes over people. Jarrell recognized this problem, and the lines from "Losses" show him hesitating between different representations of the soldier's death. The poem shifts across various modes, from "our lives wore out," which combines a poeticizing euphemism (the portrayal of death as a winding down) with cynicism (the soldiers were instruments to be used); to "our bodies lay," which poeticizes but also obscures death in order to prettify the scene ("lay" as peaceful repose, in sleep or death); to "lasted," which speaks of survival with pure cynicism; to, finally, "died," which states the case plainly but invites the question of whether plainness does in fact honestly capture the experience of death or whether it is itself an evasion of something too awful to consider.

Rather than claiming a correct depiction of the soldier's death, the poem works through a variety of possibilities only to realize the impossibility of the task itself. "Died" serves as a throwing up of the hands, with the poet resorting to the plainest word because all others have failed, and not because he has suddenly figured out the right way to talk about this subject. "Our casualties were low" gives the final blow by setting the poet's uncertainties against the confidence of propaganda's official terminology.

The poet's hesitation itself makes a strong argument. It insists that there is no right way to capture the reality of warfare, for any given depiction must be a reduction to some extent. What Jarrell gives us instead is a range of possible accounts, all inadequate in some way, but more adequate from covering such a range.

If Jarrell deemed abstraction the chief trait of propaganda, how did he avoid succumbing to its most troubling effects in his own work? Indeed, depicting war through the representative figure of the Soldier risks falling into another kind of abstraction. As was mentioned earlier, James Dickey accused Jarrell of this and thus failing to treat his subjects with the sympathy they deserved. It would be fairer to say that Jarrell uses abstract soldiers to reflect, and reflect on, the reductive, abstracting process of army life—but that he does so in a way that puts pressure on his own representation of the soldier rather than launching an attack on propaganda and what it fails to do. These are poems about the difficulties of speaking for individuals, as a poet, without resorting to abstraction.

For an example, let us turn to a slightly later poem, "Transient Barracks" (from *The Seven League Crutches* [1951]), and its account of a soldier shaving in front of a mirror, happy that he will soon return home to America. After describing the soldier (referred to as "the man"), the poet casts a glance around to "a boy in underwear," "a voice from the doorway," only to deliver the following, ambiguous lines:

> "Jesus Christ, what a field!"
> A gunner without a pass keeps saying
> To a gunner without a pass. The man
> Puts down his razor . . .[32]

The poem stages an encounter between "A gunner without a pass" and "a gunner without a pass." Both hold the same function within the army, and so both, it is suggested, are the same person in the eyes of the institution. Jarrell then surprises by cutting to "the man" at the end of the line. This raises the possibility that "the man" is one of the gunners, but if that were the case, which would he be, as the poem offers no way to differentiate between the two? Jarrell corrects that assumption in the next line by indicating that "the man" refers back to the soldier shaving ("Puts down his razor"). Still, the interpretive problems continue to pile up. The juxtaposition of two "gunners without a pass" and a single "man" might seem to individuate the latter, with the gunners as background figures and the man as a focal point. Yet "the man" is itself a vague and abstract manner of referring to a person—in its own way, far less specific than "a gunner without a pass," which at least indicates what post the men held. Impersonality poses its own set of problems. How can a writer talk about the soldier's life without resorting to types? The juxtaposition of "gunner without a pass" and "the man" shows that the poet cannot choose whether to be abstract, but only how to deploy abstraction conscientiously.

This conundrum is beautifully expressed in "Mail Call," a poem that moves between singular and plural: "The letters always just evade *the hand*," "*The soldiers* are *all* haunted by their lives," "*The soldier* simply wishes for *his* name" (emphases mine).[33] Jarrell knows these cannot be equivalent, and he was no doubt right to end with a singular rather than a plural. To go from "soldier" to "soldiers" would risk drowning out the individual experience in a group. To shift from "soldiers" to "soldier," on the other hand, gives the impression that Jarrell has managed to cut through the anonymity of army life and granted the soldier some kind of distinctiveness. This, we are told, is what the soldier longs for in the end: he "simply wishes for his name," because in hearing his name he will know that he is loved and have a renewed sense of his uniqueness as an individual. But Jarrell recognizes that this is a wish rather than a reality, and the poem begins with a singular "hand" to prevent too clean a progression from the many to the one. Either alternative has its limits. The plural form generalizes to the point of running against the combatant's desire to be recognized as an individual, while the singular makes "the soldier" into a category, not a specific person. Indeed, the sting of Jarrell's final line—"The soldier simply wishes for his name"—comes from the realization that this is precisely what the poem cannot do. Even were Jarrell to end with a name, it would be an abstract fiction intended to represent the many names that soldiers have longed to hear throughout the war.

In sum, while Jarrell thought poetry could represent some aspects of the soldier's experience (the personal, the emotional), which propaganda leaves out by virtue of its function, he also believed the poet ought to be aware of the abstracting process this entails and continually work against it. Jarrell uses a variety of methods to put pressure on his poetic depictions, and I propose to look at a few examples here. First, here is another passage from "Siegfried," this time describing the soldier's return to the United States:

And you are home, for good now almost as you wished;
If you matter, it is as little, almost, as you wished.
If it has changed, still, you have had your wish.
And are lucky, as you figured luck—are, truly, lucky.[34]

The account of the soldier's return is subjected to a series of qualifications and self-corrections. "Almost" appears twice, to temper the completeness of the soldier's satisfaction: "almost as you wished," "almost, as you wished." "If" makes whether or not "you matter" and whether or not "it has changed" uncertain, suggesting that both are true and untrue in equal measure. The soldier's return is finally deemed "lucky," only to have luck more narrowly defined ("as you figured luck") before it gets reasserted for good ("are, truly, lucky"). Jarrell's balancing act is an extended effort not to pin down the soldier's experience too simply. The poem works from the belief that individual experiences are themselves too contradictory to be summarized without betrayal. One of the ways a poet can move beyond this problem, however, is to continually rewrite, revise, and refine. Jarrell makes use of this technique as well in describing a soldier's escape from a burning plane in "A Pilot from the Carrier": "He is alone; and hangs in knowledge / Slight, separate, estranged: a lonely eye."[35] Here we find four words that almost mean the same thing, but that, of course, do not refer to the same emotion at all. There is a world of difference between feeling "alone," "separate," "estranged," or "lonely." Jarrell's decision to move from one to another suggests that even these more specific terms cannot individually capture the nuances of the pilot's emotions at this moment. Instead, he allows these shades of feeling to overlap and play off one another.

The other way that Jarrell exerts pressure on his own poetic depictions is through the use of (what I would call) near-clichés. In most instances, clichés tend toward abstraction by giving us an interpretation of the world that has been oversimplified by overuse. Whatever complexities they might have offered in an earlier form have been flattened out, leaving a phrase or image that claims universality because it is wheeled out for any number of situations. In his poems, Jarrell evokes the platitudes of war writing in order to amend them in small but important ways. An example of this process from "Gunner," a poem written in the voice of a disillusioned soldier: "Did they send me away from my cat and my wife / . . . / To a line on a plain, to a stove in a tent?"[36] "My cat and my wife" wanders near the clichés of domesticity, only to skirt them with a few odd adjustments. A cat, indeed, does not fit into the formulaic picture of married home life quite as well as a dog would, though a cat is not quite so outlandish as to disrupt it. The order in which the soldier's loved ones appear—cat before wife—is similarly provoking, and even more so that the idiosyncratic sequence does not seem intended to reveal anything about the marriage. The soldier then goes on to depict his life in the military by juxtaposing the starkness and plainness of "a stove in a tent" with an image that borders strangely on the allegorical: "a line on a plain," and its evocation of poetic writing. At the same time, even "a stove in a tent" seems peculiar as a representative example of bleak living conditions. It is both less awful than we have been made to expect (certainly than the question "Did they send me away . . . for this?" would suggest), and less emblematic than the soldier's desired effect would require. As a symbol of desolation, the stove hovers between banality and absurdity.

Such small failures are also the poem's greatest strengths. There is a sense in Jarrell's poetry that clichés lurk around every corner as soon as one attempts to describe the reality of warfare. While a poet cannot hope to circumvent cliché entirely, he can call attention to the inevitable risk, to both hold himself under scrutiny and make his readers more alert to the danger in turn. Near-clichés of the kind described here keep the risk in view while simultaneously pushing against it. For a poet so conscious of how other writers, like Auden, had become susceptible to the abstract reductions they wished to combat, this balance must have seemed the only defensible, and sustainable, position he could take.

Jarrell understood propaganda as bound by conflicting obligations. On the one hand, it was clear to him that the United States needed propaganda to rouse support to combat the Nazi regime and that the values advertised in propaganda are essential for democracy, even if they are often distorted by propaganda. Yet he also believed that propaganda should be held accountable for its abuses and excesses. The challenge Jarrell faced, successfully, was admitting to the important work of propaganda at a particular moment in history, without accepting and so succumbing to its more dubious manifestations.

3

LANGSTON HUGHES
ON
WAR PROPAGANDA
AND
RACIAL INJUSTICE

One of the most significant contributions of Langston Hughes to the development of echo and critique was his attention to the racial implications of wartime political clichés, to which his white contemporaries were largely blind. The differences between his use of echo and critique and that of Randall Jarrell are especially instructive. Like Jarrell, Hughes wrote a series of poems during the conflict in which he responded critically to the stock phrases of war propaganda, particularly those that make use of abstract values such as "truth," "freedom," or "democracy." And like Jarrell, he reflected on the discrepancy between all that these values promised and their imperfect application in society. Yet his experience as a Black man in the United States led him to a different emphasis. Even as Jarrell recognized the limits of abstraction, he continued to write in general terms about "the soldier" and "the civilian." Hughes, by contrast, was alert to how differently concepts such as "freedom" were granted (or refused) to white and Black Americans. The disparity that he wished to expose lay not between propaganda and reality broadly conceived but between propaganda and the lived reality of different citizens in the United States.

Ironically, prior to the war, critics had begun to accuse Hughes of writing poems that were more propaganda than art. In the late 1930s, as Hughes moved increasingly to the left, his poetry took on a more explicit political edge, appearing in venues that were clearly partisan. His book *A New Song* (1938), for example, was published by the International Workers Order, a mutual benefit organization with close ties to the Communist Party. Few critics reviewed the book, but those who did tended to dismiss it summarily as "leftist propaganda."[1] World War II shifted the general attitude toward mass persuasion. Hughes was commissioned by government agencies to write propaganda in support of the troops, like many other writers, and this did no damage to his reputation. Still, after the war, his earlier political commitments came under scrutiny once again. In 1953, the House Committee on Un-American Activities called Hughes to testify, accusing him of treason and branding his poetry as "Communist propaganda."[2]

Hughes's relationship with propaganda was far more complicated than his contemporaries wished to acknowledge. His war poems repeatedly challenged propaganda's tendency to deceive and abuse. But Hughes was also part of a tradition in African American thought that saw propaganda as an important tool in advancing civil rights. For W. E. B. Du Bois in "Criteria of Negro Art" (1926), "all art is propaganda and ever must be, despite the wailing of the purists" because real art works in the service of equality and justice: "I stand in utter shamelessness and say that whatever art I have for writing has been used always for propaganda for gaining the right of black folk to love and enjoy. I do not care a damn for any art that is not used for propaganda. But I do care when propaganda is confined to one side while the other is stripped and silent."[3] Propaganda is not objectionable in and of itself but only when used to block competing claims. Du Bois anticipates defenses of propaganda that became popular with the advent of World War II, as a way of distinguishing democracies like the United States (which would soon make use of propaganda) from dictatorships in Europe.[4] But his distinction is animated specifically by a concern for minority voices and the fear that these voices are the ones that risk being silenced when propaganda gets misused.

Hughes, writing a month after the end of World War II for the *Chicago Defender,* took up DuBois's connection between propaganda and justice, though with a different emphasis:

> The things of which man can be proud, the beauty that he can really enjoy, are born only of truth, or the attempt to attain truth. That is why art in its essence is a path to truth. Propaganda is a path toward more to eat. That the two may be inextricably mixed is not to be denied. That they may often be one and the same is certainly true. But that the greatest art is also the greatest truth—and at the same time therefore the greatest propaganda for a good life for everybody—is beyond the possibility of sane denial.[5]

The proximity of "truth" and "beauty" revises John Keats's famous statement in "Ode on a Grecian Urn" ("Beauty is truth, truth beauty") by bringing it down into the realm of everyday necessity. The striking connection here is between "truth" (the end point of art) and "a good life" (the end point of propaganda). If art leads one to truth, and truth is the happiness of a life well lived, then art cannot so easily be separated from propaganda. Hughes stops just short of linking them definitively ("That they *may* often be one and the same is certainly true"), but his polemical attitude is evident in the starkness of "a path toward more to eat," which brings the abstractions "beauty" and "truth" back down from the contemplative miasma where those terms often reside.

The efficacy of Hughes's argument depends to a large degree on simplification, of course: there is no acknowledgment of propaganda that does not advocate for a better life or that claims to offer some people a better life to the detriment of others. Most surprisingly, Hughes appears to set aside propaganda by the government and the military. As the phrase "a path toward more to eat" suggests, he has in mind only the political materials produced by individuals, labor unions, and civil rights groups.

The goal is to reframe propaganda, not as the impersonal manipulation of institutions but as the advocacy of real people in specific circumstances fighting for a better life. Hughes found this redefinition and simplification necessary as a way of defending the political poetry that he and other African Americans were writing.

Throughout his life, Hughes grounded the political nature of his poetry in his own lived experience, and framed the connection between art and propaganda as a matter of necessity in his particular situation. In a 1951 interview with Rochelle Gibson, he noted: "I have often been termed a propaganda or protest writer. . . . That designation has probably grown out of the fact that I write about what I know best, and being a Negro in this country is tied up with difficulties that cause one to protest naturally."[6] Hughes describes a chain of necessity. Because life as a Black man in the United States is defined by difficulties, it is only "natural" that he would wish to protest; and because he is a poet, it is to be expected that the poems he writes will be labeled propaganda. That Hughes was conscious of this rhetorical footwork becomes evident when his interview is set against the following passage from *I Wonder as I Wander: An Autobiographical Journey*, published five years later:

> To me as a writer, it was especially interesting to observe how art of all sorts—writing, painting, the theatre—was being utilized as a weapon against the evils of the past. To be sure art, put to such use, often degenerated into propaganda. But even propaganda in talented hands took on dramatic dimensions. In Tashkent, talented, Russian directors were using all the folk elements of Uzbek music, poetry and dance in aiding to create the Uzbek national theatre where there had been none before.[7]

This time, Hughes accepts the common pejorative meaning of the term "propaganda," conceding that political art "often degenerated" into that category. He no longer speaks of it as an honorable fight for a better life, leaning instead on the usual criticism of agitation and manipulation. The key distinction now lies between propaganda in "talented" hands and (presumably) less talented hands. Good artists can make propaganda something more than it would otherwise be.

World War II offers an especially interesting chapter in the history of Hughes's relationship with propaganda. Like many others, Hughes deemed it important to galvanize support in the fight against fascism. He wrote a number of pieces that echoed the rhetoric of military propaganda and encouraged readers in America to see themselves as integral to the "war effort." One such example is the poem "Fourth of July Thought" (1942), which concludes with: "The HOME FRONT is YOU!"[8] The capitalization and exclamation mark bring the poem to a dramatic close by imitating the visual style of propaganda posters. While "The HOME FRONT is YOU" may not be drawn from any actual poster, it does evoke slogans like "I WANT YOU FOR U.S. ARMY," most famously displayed beneath a drawing of Uncle Sam pointing at the observer. "The war front" and "the home front" were real stock phrases of wartime political discourse, but the poem does not function as echo and critique, since it does not critique the language that it takes up. Instead, Hughes uses the phrases to create a new slogan that would fit quite seamlessly on the posters released by the public communications office of the American military. There is little room for qualification, critical distance, or even any hint of irony. The tone from the start of the poem is one of total seriousness, from the opening command "Remember," to the sentimental image of the "Soldiers of Democracy" as angels "Guard[ing] our earth and sky," and the finger-wagging solemnity of "Those of us who stay at home / Have grave duties, too."

World War II is one of the only periods in which we see Hughes aligning his poetry with the goals of the American government rather than standing in opposition to a hostile majority culture. In fact, Hughes accepted a number of commissions from the government to write war propaganda. But the prejudice he encountered in his dealings with government officials no doubt encouraged the more critical responses to propaganda in his poetry. After writing a script for the morale-boosting radio show *Keep 'Em Rolling*, Hughes was told that writers did not get paid to contribute to the war effort through their talents, as such work was simply a mark of patriotism. He later found out that white writers were in fact getting paid for their scripts.[9] The following year, in 1943, Hughes lent his hand to a different political event: the "Negro Freedom Rally," held at Madison Square Garden. The script that Hughes wrote for this event, titled *For This We Fight,* is important in considering Hughes's wartime echo and critique on two counts. First, the script showed Hughes's interest in connecting the Allied fight against fascism with the African American fight against segregation in the United States, a move that, as Joseph McLaren has noted, mirrored the strategies of the NAACP and the National Urban League.[10] Like other African American thinkers, Hughes hoped that the war would, to quote Arnold Rampersad, "exert enormous pressure against segregation."[11] Second, *For This We Fight* takes on key stock phrases from military propaganda, but the approach helps to distinguish Hughes's echo and critique in poetry from his work in drama. The script warrants a brief look before turning to the poems.

At the end of the show, the figure of the Soldier plays on, and with, Franklin D. Roosevelt's "Four Freedoms": freedom of speech, freedom of worship, freedom from want, and freedom from fear. While Roosevelt first outlined these in his January 1941 State of the Union address, the phrases were repurposed in various propaganda after the United States entered the war in December of that same year.[12] Hughes expands the scope of these liberties in order to suggest that they have not been granted equally to all Americans.

> Freedom of worship, freedom of press,
> Freedom from want and freedom from fear—
> For this we fight! For this we fight!
> Freedom to vote and freedom to work,
> Freedom to speak and freedom to hear—
> For this we fight! For this we fight!
> America, our homeland,
> Ever dear will be,
> That's why we want America
> For ALL men to be free!
> Let's put an end to the color bar!
> Let's put an end to the Jim Crow car!
> For the right to be men
> In this land we defend—
> !!!!! FOR THIS WE FIGHT !!!!![13]

Hughes makes his case first by reaching beyond Roosevelt's four free-doms to other liberties that, it is implied, follow from them: freedom to vote, work, speak, and hear. In turn, that expansion sets up the de-mand that such freedoms to be applied equally to all Americans. The speech ends with a call to end segregation and a reassertion of the show's title, a play on the title of Frank Capra's 1942 war propaganda film *Why We Fight*.[14]

The purpose and mechanics of this monologue are clear, and indeed that very simplicity is a mark of the form and genre in which Hughes was writing. Unlike readers of poetry, rally audiences do not have the luxury of hearing a line twice or going back to an earlier point in the performance. Scriptwriters, especially in the context of a political rally such as the one that Hughes participated in, must ensure that their ideas are communicated in the moment. The techniques that Hughes employs to critique Roosevelt's "four freedoms" are thus exceedingly simple and directly mirror his political argument. Moreover, the sheer repetitious-ness of this passage evokes the repetitions of slogans and political chants (appropriately for the Negro Freedom Rally). Hughes creates new pro-paganda out of propaganda which revealed fundamental inequalities in the United States. His goal, in this instance, was to galvanize rather than to invite reflection.

The poems in which Hughes makes use of echo and critique also have political arguments to make, and they communicate these clearly. But the fact that readers can slow down, look back, and start a text over again from the beginning enabled him to perform more subtle and complex work in poetry than in drama. Hughes repeatedly layers a variety of tech-niques within a single poem, and it is worth identifying his most import-ant ones here in brief before turning to specific examples. First, he often makes use of rhyme in order to emphasize a contrast between the claims of propaganda and the everyday experience of African Americans. In this, he resembles Randall Jarrell, whose poem "A Lullaby" yokes the propagandist phrase "to fight for freedom and the State" with the morbidity of "six men within six feet." Second, he deploys and withholds capitalization, espe-cially around value terms such as *Freedom* and *Democracy,* so as to reveal discrepancies in how these ideas are touted and applied in reality. There are echoes of this in Jarrell, too, with the scattering of "Freedom" into a host of lowercase "freedoms" in "Port of Embarkation." The third major technique has to do with persona, and it is here that Hughes introduces a new approach, absent not only in Jarrell but also in Auden. Hughes frames many of the poems echoing and critiquing war propaganda in the voice of a lower-class Black everyman. Auden and Jarrell, by contrast, tended to use the lyric voice of the poet ("September 1, 1939") or an omniscient voice ("Spain"), which at times evoked the impersonal perspective of bureaucracy ("The Unknown Citizen"). Hughes's decision to write from the point of view of a working-class African American was crucial to his political argument, though, because it allowed him to test the rhetoric of war propaganda against the experience of an individual excluded by that rhetoric. His speakers are typically ironic about propaganda's hypocrisy, expressing surprise that "Freedom" and "Democracy" are not fully granted to them, even as Hughes makes it clear that they have suffered too much to be in any way surprised. That irony is shared both by the speakers and the poet himself.

The complex interplay of voice, tone, rhyme, and typography fosters a skeptical relationship with language, beyond even what *For This We Fight* could accomplish because of its function within the context of a political rally. Hughes invites us to be critical of seemingly authoritative statements and the intentions they disguise. The following pages consider a series of poems, published between 1940 and 1943, that illustrate subtle evolutions while emphasizing the consistency of his echo and critique. It is important to note that Hughes produced much of his war propaganda during this same period as well. ("Fourth of July Thought," for example, appeared in 1942.) The following poems do not show Hughes reforming and renouncing such work but rather building a critical counterpoint to the propaganda he was producing at the time.

Surprisingly, in light of the poems that soon followed, Hughes first made use of echo and critique during World War II to discourage American military intervention. The poem "Comment on War," published in the *Crisis* in June 1940, pushes back against the abstract term "truth" as the common justification for war's objective and the incentive for civilians to join or condone the fight.

Let us kill off youth
For the sake of *truth*.

We who are old know what truth is—
Truth is a bundle of vicious lies
Tied together and sterilized—
A war-maker's bait for unwise youth
To kill off each other
For the sake of
Truth.[15]

The opening stanza issues a provocative statement, designed to elicit shock and disapproval from its readers, and culminating in the word "truth." The use of italics suggests both how much is justified on its head and how meager that word seems when set against all that is performed under its name. The brevity of the lines and the clarity of the rhyme together create a singsong rhythm, wholly ironic in this context. The second stanza picks up on that irony and makes explicit points that are implicit in the opening sentence. Chief among these is the rather straightforward charge of doublespeak: the government and military may claim that we need to sacrifice our youth to truth, but in actuality that truth is "a bundle of vicious lies," as the motive for war is always more complex, and less honorable, than propaganda may claim.

The argument is simple, but the most complex and interesting work in the poem occurs in the last four lines. By placing "youth" at the end of a line, Hughes creates anticipation as to when "truth," its partner in rhyme, will reappear. In fact, he delays the word until the last line of the poem, where it is italicized and presented alone. "*Truth*" is also capitalized, and while this simply follows the convention of capitalizing the first letter of each line, the capitalization puts additional emphasis and pressure on this term. Hughes's typographical choices have a double effect. On the one hand, the poem implies that "truth" has been emptied of all its meaning, so the italics and capitalization come with a note of irony. On the other, the emphasis suggests that the word still has power, specifically over the "unwise youth," for whom Truth remains grand and unquestionable.

Hughes's focus on the gap between rhetoric and reality in this poem is similar to Jarrell's own war poetry, which also takes propaganda to task for deceptively evoking abstract values. Like Jarrell as well, he generalizes the soldiers by referring to them simply as "youth," without any distinguishing markers beyond age. But of course, Hughes knew that the soldiers' experiences were not identical, and that the unjust treatment of racial minorities in society was also apparent in the military. Within a year, he sharpened his echo and critique to ponder the more specific incongruity between America and Europe's stated dedication to liberty and the unequal application of those freedoms among their own people. The goal, then, was to expose the hypocrisy of claiming to defend freedom against the threat of totalitarian regimes while maintaining discrimination toward African Americans and Black people across the world.

Hughes confronted this paradox even before the United States officially entered the war in January 1942. "Explain It, Please," published in *Amsterdam News* on June 14, 1941, critiques British propaganda through a network of contrasts and failed rhymes. The poem begins with a striking double opposition:

> I see by the papers
> What seems mighty funny to me.
> The British are fighting for freedom
> But India ain't free.[16]

The first contrast occurs between "me" and "free." Like the citizens of India, the speaker is far from "free." The simplicity and clarity of the rhyme underlines, ironically, the distance between the two, as the musical connection implies that they ought to be linked in reality. The second, more discreet contrast is to be found between "freedom" (an abstract noun) and "free" (an adjective). The chief difference lies between liberty as a concept and a lived experience. Hughes suggests that what the British have been fighting for is the idea of freedom rather than its actual fulfillment, which logically should prompt them to grant independence to their colonies.

As the poem continues, Hughes reinforces and expands the implicit parallel between the plight of Black people across the world:

The colored weeklies tell me
In the British colonies
The white man stands on his two feet
But the black man's on his knees
And they tell me that in Africa
The color line's drawn tight,
So when the English holler freedom
Can it be that they are right?

The "color line" extends from India to Africa and, importantly, the United States. The phrase itself, made famous by Frederick Douglass and later W. E. B. Du Bois, establishes a connection between the racism suffered by Black people in the British colonies and in America.[17] Similarly, the reference to the "colored weeklies" affirms what the dialect of the opening four lines implied, that the speaker of the poem is African American and that the hypocrisy he decries is not limited to England alone.

The term "freedom" recurs several times in the poem, but tellingly it is never rhymed and so remains marginal both musically and symbolically. In the last four lines, it is set in a haunting parallel with the word "smoke":

Course there's a mighty lot of fog and smoke,
But I'm trying hard to see
How folks can have a mouth full of freedom—
And a handful of dung for me.

Here, too, the sheer simplicity of the rhyme on "see" and "me" yokes "smoke" and "freedom" together by contrast. The absence of rhyme creates a discordant effect, even as the two words share just enough letters for us to read them as a pair (*smoke, freedom*); and, indeed, the point is that the concept of freedom has very much become a "lot of fog and smoke," concealing the real injustices and inequalities on which England and America are founded. The final occurrence of "me," by rhyming with "see," crystallizes the speaker's reckoning with this global hypocrisy, and the clarity he achieves in the poem's final moments.

Four months later, Hughes published a second poem where he directed this critique more narrowly at those arguing that the United States should enter the war. "Southern Negro Speaks," which appeared in *Opportunity* in October 1941, deploys the same voice and irony found in "Explain It, Please." The speaker pretends to be confused by the unequal application of "freedom" and "democracy," even as the poet makes it clear that the speaker has suffered too much disappointment to feel any surprise. Again, Hughes plays with rhyme to underline the discrepancy between America's stated values and the lived experience of racial minorities in the United States. But he also advances his analysis further by fleshing out a paradox: namely, that the stock phrases of propaganda still have power over people, even if they appear to be insubstantial.

The first four lines echo the techniques used in "Explain It, Please" by pairing abstractions and pronouns in an implicit contrast:

> I reckon they must have
> Forgotten about me
> When I hear them say they gonna
> Save Democracy.[18]

The contrast is reinforced by scale. On one side there is "me": a lowercase monosyllable dwarfed even further by the three-syllable "Forgotten" looming over it at the head of its line. On the other stands the capitalized authority of "Democracy," which turns the whole line into a unified slogan ("Save Democracy") and brings the first sentence to a close. The contrast expresses the speaker's feeling of smallness and vulnerability before the abstractions that so dominate public discourse and thought. The idea of Democracy is too potent to concede that it has excluded some people from its realm, including the poet. The lines that follow trace a gradual shift in the speaker's attitude toward these abstract values, as he gradually gains control over them:

> Funny thing about white folks
> Wanting to go fight
> Way over in Europe
> For freedom and light
> When right here in Alabama—
> Lord have mercy on me!—

They declare I'm a Fifth Columnist
If I say the word, *Free.*

Hughes echoes the common propagandist phrase, "to fight for freedom," which had caught Jarrell's imagination as well. Whereas Jarrell revealed the institutions that the phrase actually aimed to defend ("fight for freedom and the State"), Hughes's critique focuses instead on the insubstantial nature of these abstractions in a society that does not grant them to its citizens equally. "For freedom and light": the addition of "light" makes a mockery of the phrase and of American claims of "freedom" more generally, implying that such phrases do not carry any weight. But the recurrence of a rhyme on "me," this time with the capitalized and italicized word *"Free,"* transforms the speaker's relation to these abstract terms. "Free" has now been separated from the stock phrases where it had been rendered ineffective and now stands both as an adjective asserting the speaker's independence and a verb demanding political freedom that he does not yet fully possess. Even though "me" appears in a small prayer that typically expresses self-correction, lament, or regret ("Lord have mercy on me!"), the use of an exclamation mark in conjunction with the rhyme on *"Free"* makes the pronoun boldly assertive. In short, the speaker takes ownership of the abstractions that had seemed to him empty clichés and gives them an urgent vitality by requiring that the United States abide by its principles.

The remainder of the poem tracks a sudden, dispiriting return to the realities of life in the United States. The very next line, "Jim Crow all around me," introduces yet another rhyme on "me," but the recurrence of the pronoun is of a different tenor. What the line describes—the constant encroachment of racist policies literally surrounding the speaker—curbs the assertive power that the pronoun had gained from its association with *"Free."* In fact, the abruptness of this rhyme, after the staggered ABCB scheme of the previous twelve lines, only reinforces the sense that the speaker's bid for freedom has been curtailed. As in the poem's opening, "me" is visually diminished by standing opposite a capitalized "Jim Crow" at the head of the line. The phrase referring to racist policies in the United States reappears at the end of the poem with even greater force:

Cause I sure don't understand
What the meaning can be
When folks talk about freedom—
And Jim Crow me?

"Jim Crow" has now become an active verb, rather than a personification, directly impacting "me." The immediate juxtaposition carries a troubling undercurrent of violence, evoking all the pressures and threats to which the speaker is subject. "*Free*" has reverted back to the abstract nominalization "freedom" and lost its capitalization, becoming merely a topic of "talk" rather than a state of being the speaker can assert or require.

After the United States entered the war in December 1941, Hughes grew more assertive in his rejection of cliché and his demand that America live up to the abstract values that it peddled in propaganda. One example is "The Black Man Speaks," a poem from *Jim Crow's Last Stand* (1943), where Hughes once again uses rhyme to important effect. The first three stanzas read:

I swear to the Lord
I still can't see
Why Democracy means
Everybody but me.

I swear to my soul
I can't understand
Why Freedom don't apply
To the black man.

I swear, by gum,
I really don't know
Why in the name of Liberty
You treat me so.[19]

Conspicuously, none of the abstract values rhyme. The poet buries "Democracy" and "Freedom" within the third lines of their respective stanzas. Even when he does finally place a value term at the end of a line with "Liberty," he still leaves that word unrhymed. The lack of musical consonance is meant to represent how ineffective they are, how far removed from the realities of lived experience. The effect is made all the more striking by the clarity of the rhymes that Hughes does include (all are monosyllables except for one) and their semantic resonance. Indeed, the pairing of "see" and "me," as well as of "understand" and "black man," emphasizes the words and creates a bold countermusic to the speaker's apparent confusion ("I still can't see," "I can't understand"). This is a self (*me*) who demands to be *seen*, a *black man* who demands that the reader *understand*. The speaker confronts his audience with the sheer plainness of his language, against which capitalized abstractions such as "Democracy" seem painfully out of touch.

The final stanza presents a rhetorical question which advocates for change and mirrors that change symbolically in its form:

> If we're fighting to create
> A free world tomorrow,
> Why not end *right now*
> Old Jim Crow's sorrow?

Previous stanzas were structured around a simple ABCB rhyme scheme. The final stanza follows the scheme to some extent with a full rhyme on "tomorrow" and "sorrow." However, the introduction of one additional eye rhyme with the italicized "*right now*" disrupts the pattern, creating a visual chain of *ow* words. The fact that the poem's established rhyme scheme is broken by "*right now*" specifically matters, since the phrase conveys the speaker's urgent plea for systemic change. Old patterns can no longer hold, and the poem symbolically enacts the changes that it demands through its form.

The boldness of Hughes's poetry after the United States entered the war is best illustrated by the way that he confronted Franklin Roosevelt's speech rhetoric. "How About It, Dixie," published in *New Masses* in October 1942 and then later reprinted in *Jim Crow's Last Stand*, torques Roosevelt's "Four Freedoms," which he would later echo in *For This We Fight* as well. The comparison between the poem and the play is instructive, since it reveals the distinctiveness of Hughes's response in verse as opposed to other forms. "How About It, Dixie" begins, like several of his other poems that make use of echo and critique, by playing with pronouns.

> The President's Four Freedoms
> Appeal to me.
> I would like to see those Freedoms
> Come to be.
>
> If you believe
> In the Four Freedoms, too,
> Then share 'em with me—
> Don't keep 'em all for you.[20]

The first stanza presents a now familiar contrast, between the authority of capitalized "Freedoms" on the one hand (which dominate by appearing twice in an identical rhyme), and the smallness of the pronoun "me" on the other. The sheer difference in scale helps to see the speaker, despite his profession of humility ("I would like to see"), as quite bold rather than meek. As in Hughes's other World War II poems, the line endings serve to test individual experience against the nation's stated principles. The poet's energies are then directed in the second stanza to an addressee, imagined as a representative white person or white Americans as a group (the pronoun could be singular or plural). "The Four Freedoms" retreat, allowing other words to take prominence at the end of the lines. The key pair, though, is not "too" and "you," but "me" and "you," placed in direct parallel. The absence of rhyme reinforces the contrast, bringing home the idea that one's experience of "freedom" in America depends on who "I" am, on who "you" are. The word "Freedom" recurs two stanzas later, this time in opposition to civil rights figures from the United States and beyond.

> You can't lock up Gandhi,
> Club Roland Hayes,
> Then make fine speeches
> About Freedom's ways.

It is striking to move from the first stanza, where two "Freedoms" loomed over a diminutive "me," to this fourth stanza, where the capitalized names of Gandhi and Roland Hayes are made equal to such abstract terms. The visual parallel serves Hughes's argument: namely, that while most speeches use liberty only as an empty gesture, some individuals have embodied this value and, through their actions, kept it from becoming merely rhetoric. The poem ends by folding in another stock phrase of wartime public discourse:

> Freedom's not just
> To be won Over There.
> It means Freedom at home, too—
> Now—*right here!*

The capital *O* and *T* signal that this is a borrowed phrase. A shorthand for Europe during the war, "Over There" conveys the aura of mystery and uncertainty that surrounded the continent in the eyes of most Americans, even as it also betrays a desire to keep the realities of the war at a distance, in a mythical other land whose violence will never reach the shores of the United States. Hughes turns against that evasion and distancing, toward an immediate conflict: the fight for freedom that must be won "now," "*right here!*" The latter phrase appears in crouching italics, after a series of dashes, and topped by an exclamation mark. The poem gathers speed as it reaches an end, so that taken together these typographical choices underline the urgency of the cause. Hughes asserts that, for Freedom to really "mean" something, the United States must make systemic changes and ensure that the lived experience of all its citizens fulfills the values put forward in its political rhetoric.

It is an argument that Hughes made with regard to Roosevelt's "Four Freedoms" in *For This We Fight* as well. Still, the echo and critique in "How About It, Dixie" differs in execution and in its broader implications. Both the play and the poem are works of public advocacy. But by trying to galvanize its immediate audience, which can hear the words only once, the play does not question the rhetoric itself so much as demand its wider application. No wonder, then, that Hughes creates his own slogans as addenda to the phrases that were already in circulation:

"Freedom to vote and freedom to work, / Freedom to speak and freedom to hear— / For this we fight! For this we fight!" On the other hand, the poem's layering of techniques—a complex interplay of rhyme, typography, contrast—fosters a more critical relation to the very language through which are rights are defended, granted, or withheld. His readers are asked not just to demand more of political rhetoric but also to scrutinize that rhetoric and question its meaning and uses with greater skepticism. This is something that could be said of all Hughes's wartime poems that deploy echo and critique.

There is one other important caveat, and it is one that connects Hughes and Jarrell. Like Jarrell, Hughes stops short of claiming that we ought to do away with concepts like "Freedom" on the grounds that they had been too vitiated. On the contrary, he deemed it essential to take the words themselves seriously and not become so cynical as to simply mock or reject the values they represent. Several poems in *Jim Crow's Last Stand* state this clearly, and their inclusion in this volume alongside "The Black Man Speaks" and "How About It, Dixie" makes them fitting companions to the poems of echo and critique. In the final lines of "Freedom," for example, Hughes writes:

> I tire so of hearing people say,
> *Let things take their course.*
> *Tomorrow is another day.*
> I do not need my freedom when I'm dead.
> I cannot live on tomorrow's bread.
> >Freedom
> >Is a strong seed
> >Planted
> >In a great need.
> >I live here, too.
> >I want my freedom
> >Just as you.[21]

The shift from long to short lines, paired with the indentation, slows the poem down and prompts a heightening of attention. The drag of frustration and despair ("I do not need my freedom when I'm dead. / I cannot live on tomorrow's bread.") gives way to intense, focused assertations in the face of adversity. The effect is reinforced by the choice of verbs, which connote states of being ("is," "live") and then desire or necessity ("want"), and the isolation of the capitalized word "Freedom" within its own line. Indeed, it is this word that marks a shift, from the world of fact and the pressures of the immediate present ("tomorrow's bread"), to universal values and metaphor, which allows the poet to envision their fulfillment ("a strong seed / Planted / In a great need"). The capacity for poetry to imagine an alternative world where those abstract terms are realized itself grants him some degree of freedom, even if he must eventually return to the world of facts and demands that promise to be honored in reality. "I want my freedom / Just as you."

Another poem, also titled "Freedom," personifies this abstraction to assert its resilience. The poem is made up of five stanzas. The first three, all beginning with the line "Some folks think," relate the assumptions of those who believe "freedom" can be defeated by burning books, arresting civil rights leaders, or lynching African Americans. The last two stanzas counter those suppositions firmly:

But Freedom
Stands up and laughs
In their faces
And says,

You'll never kill me![22]

Even if this particular poem does not investigate its key abstraction critically, it does still share with Hughes's echo and critique the belief that the word "Freedom" should be treated with more respect, not less. Throughout all his wartime poetry, Hughes wrote in the hope that a more critical approach to the stock phrases of public discourse would help pave the way for a broader political reckoning. In order for these terms to be used honestly, society would need to align itself more closely with its stated values. By holding public discourse accountable, Hughes hoped to bring about changes which would ensure that "Freedom" and "Democracy" say what they mean and that society uphold these values in reality.

4

CLAUDE McKAY
ON THE
POLITICAL CLICHÉS
OF THE
HOME FRONT

As we have seen, World War II proved to be the defining event in the development of echo and critique after Auden began to adopt this method in the years leading up to the conflict. Yet in the history of echo and critique's postwar expansion, Claude McKay matters especially because the rhetorical context he responded to was not, in fact, the war. Whereas Jarrell and Hughes examined how military propaganda beautified or erased the real-life experiences of soldiers and African Americans, McKay focused on the stock phrases surrounding domestic politics in the United States and studied the way that these obscured or distorted social realities. The phrases that interested him most fell under two categories: first, the nationalist rhetoric of community and shared values; and, second, the rhetoric of protest in support of labor rights or civil rights. McKay's focus matters because it is so easy, in retrospect, for the war to dominate our view of the political situation in the United States and the rhetoric that poets critiqued. McKay's work is a record of the domestic struggle around inequality that persisted in this period, and how poets sought to confront its ramifications in the realm of political language.

Like Jarrell and Hughes, McKay was fascinated by propaganda. But his relation to mass political persuasion was, arguably, even more complicated than that of either of his contemporaries. From 1919 (when he began a three-year stint as coeditor of the socialist magazine the *Liberator* with Max Eastman) to 1928 (when he published his first novel, *Home to Harlem*), McKay embraced propaganda as a necessary tool in combating racism and colonialism. In a letter to Francine Budgen from August 1920, he noted, casually but with obvious excitement: "I am merely doing my bit of propaganda to offset that of the anti-Negro Americans, the colonial whites, and prejudiced Englishmen."[1] His most notable public statement on propaganda during this time, though, is the essay "Soviet Russia and the Negro," published in *Crisis* in December 1923. In it, McKay begins with a bold assertion intended to provoke: "The label of propaganda will be affixed to what I say here. I shall not mind; propaganda has now come into its respectable rights and I am proud of being a propagandist."[2] He then expands the meaning of propaganda to encompass any work of art that seeks a political outcome. He does so by tracing how his literary taste evolved over time. After devoting most of his boyhood to the "gilt-washed artificiality" of *style for style's sake* (as exemplified by Oscar Wilde's *The Picture of Dorian Gray*), he "lighted on one of Milton's greatest sonnets that was pure propaganda and a widening horizon revealed that some of the finest spirits of modern literature—Voltaire, Hugo, Heine, Swift, Shelly, Byron, Tolstoy, Ibsen—had carried the taint of propaganda." That broader view "swung me away from the childish age of the enjoyment of creative work for pleasurable curiosity to another extreme where I have always sought for the motivating force or propaganda intent that underlies all literature of interest."[3] Such a narrative accomplishes two things. First, the conflation of "propaganda" with the vagueness of "a motivating force" sweeps under that heading all works that have political ideas to communicate. Second, the biographical narrative enables McKay to peg as "childish" any interest in art distinct from politics. "Another extreme" concedes there may be limits to his new perspective on art, but the gesture seems largely empty. Those limits are never spelled out, and the rest of the essay advocates for the importance of propaganda both as a tool for progress ("American Negroes are not as yet deeply permeated with the mass movement spirit and so fail to see the importance of organized propaganda") and as a threat that had to be reckoned with ("It was not until I first came to Europe in 1919 that I came to a full realization and understanding of the effectiveness of the insidious propaganda in general that is maintained against the Negro race").[4]

The political poetry that McKay wrote at the turn of the 1920s carries out the principle that good art should have a "propaganda intent." Yet it also betrays some unease as to what such writing would require. The most famous poem from this era, "If We Must Die" (first printed in the *Liberator* in July 1919), may appear to fit neatly in the category of propaganda thanks to its rousing oratorical tone and rhythm, evident in the opening lines: "If we must die, let it not be like hogs / Hunted and penned in an inglorious spot, / While round us bark the mad and hungry dogs."[5] Wayne F. Cooper reads this poem as a direct response to the East St. Louis Riots of 1917, during which a white mob murdered between 39 and 150 African Americans.[6] But McKay is careful to generalize his claims so that they cannot be tied too specifically to any one cause. He casts the players allegorically as animals ("hogs," "mad and hungry dogs") and at the same time frames the conflict in terms that can either be taken literally or metaphorically depending on the context, as in the final line of the poem, where he encourages his followers to remain strong: "Pressed to the wall, dying, but fighting back." The poem's original venue reinforces its shift toward abstraction. As Tyrone Tillery notes, it matters that "If We Must Die" first appeared in a white radical magazine, as it indicates that "the poem had been intended for a wider audience than just the black community, few of whom read the *Liberator*."[7] Jean Wagner celebrates that broad applicability as a mark of the poet's generosity: "Along with the will to resistance of black Americans that it expresses, [the poem] voices also the will of oppressed peoples of every age who, whatever their race and wherever their region, are fighting with their backs against the wall to win freedom."[8] That is certainly a fortuitous side effect of the abstractions, yet the use of allegory reveals a fear that the poem would be cheapened if tied to a particular cause, a specific context involving real people. "If We Must Die" has "force" but no actual "motivation"; a "propaganda intent" but no target. It remains divorced from any one historical situation. Tillery argues that "what he desired most in 1919 was to be the 'individual soul' who sought what was noblest and best in the life of the individual."[9] That desire to be an "individual" is, in effect, a desire to stand apart from the messy complications of society and history—arguably the pressing concern behind "If We Must Die." But in a political poem such as this, the only way for him to stand apart was (paradoxically) to universalize through abstraction.

The most important shift in McKay's attitude toward propaganda came about in 1928, with the critical response to his debut novel *Home to Harlem*. The book stirred up controversy because of its unvarnished portrayal of African American life. The most high-profile critique, and also the most severe, came from W. E. B. Du Bois: "*Home to Harlem* for the most part nauseates me, and after the dirtier parts of its filth I feel distinctly like taking a bath. . . . It looks as though McKay has set out to cater to that prurient demand on the part of white folk for a portrayal in Negroes of the utter licentiousness which conventional civilization holds white folk back from enjoying—if enjoyment it can be called."[10] This hurt McKay badly. To defend himself, he took up the mantle of universality, declaring himself a stylist as opposed to a propagandist. As he wrote to Du Bois in a private letter that same year:

My motive for writing was simply that I began in my boyhood to be an artist in words and I have stuck to that in spite of the contrary forces and colors of life that I have had to contend against through various adventures, mistakes, successes, strength and weakness of body that the artist-soul, more or less, has to pass through. Certainly I sympathize with and even pity you for not understanding my motive, because you have been forced from a normal career to enter a special field of racial propaganda and, honorable though that field may be, it has precluded you from contact with real life, for propaganda is fundamentally but a one-sided idea of life. Therefore I should not be surprised when you mistake the art of life for nonsense and try to pass off propaganda as life in art![11]

On one side stands the "artist in words," whose subject is "real life" in all its complexity, and on the other stands the more specialized author of "racial propaganda," who can only capture part of reality. McKay's rhetorical move here is to take aestheticism, which he himself had criticized as overly self-contained, and assert that this philosophy does in fact put the artist in touch with the particulars of "real life." McKay returned to this opposition several times in the ensuing years. In the 1932 essay "The Negro Writer to His Critics," he lamented the particular scrutiny that Black writers faced from Black critics as to the proper depiction of African Americans in art:

> This peculiar racial opinion constitutes a kind of censorship of what is printed about the Negro. No doubt it had its origin in the laudable efforts of intelligent Negro groups to protect their race from the slander of its detractors after Emancipation, and grew until it crystalized into racial consciousness. The pity is that these leaders of racial opinion should also be in the position of sole arbiters of intellectual and artistic things within the Negro world. For although they may be excellent persons worthy of all respect and eminently right in their purpose, they often do not distinguish between the task of propaganda and the work of art.[12]

McKay then applies this distinction to his own work, arguing that his early political poems were read incorrectly according to the terms of propaganda. Looking back to "If We Must Die," he writes: "The poem was an outgrowth of the intense emotional experience I was living through (no doubt with thousands of other Negroes) in those days."[13] This is a variation on McKay's idea of "the art of life," here defined more narrowly as the poet's own life. The goal was not to advocate or attack but simply to reflect his individual state of mind at a particular moment. The fact that others shared in this perspective is not seen as especially relevant. African American critics, however, read the poem along cruder utilitarian lines (or so McKay posited): "To them a poem that voiced the deep-rooted instinct of self-preservation seemed merely a daring piece of impertinence."[14] Propaganda finds itself downgraded from a "motivating force" (lending the work shape, meaning, and energy) to "a daring piece of impertinence": a futile provocation that (he claims) does not interest him at all.

In the years leading up to the war, his public attitude relaxed considerably. As evident in his memoirs *A Long Way from Home* (1937), he began to speak comfortably about the way propaganda appealed to him in youth: "Because of my eclectic approach to literature and my unorthodox idea of life, I developed a preference for the less conservative literary organs. *The Masses* was one of the magazines which attracted me when I came from out West to New York in 1914. I liked its slogans, its makeup, and above all, its cartoons."[15] "Slogans" gets folded into a list of qualities culminating in "cartoons," which are given preference and so diminish the apparent force of "slogans." They are not presented as an essential tool for justice, but nor are they lamented as a cheapening of thought, "a one-sided idea of life." Throughout the book, McKay speaks of his support for propaganda in the past tense, as in: "I said I thought that the only place where illegal and secret radical propaganda was necessary was among the Negroes of the South"[16] He also says that he was glad to get away from a political culture that so prized mass persuasion. He describes his time in Paris fondly because "it was like taking a holiday after living in the atmosphere of the high-pressure propaganda spirit of the new Russia."[17]

McKay's self-portrait deserves some degree of skepticism. His tone in alluding to his past beliefs is cool but also a tad forced. He seems eager not to fully own—and reckon with—his earlier defenses of propaganda by framing them as symptoms of immaturity. This is, in essence, the same strategy he had used to dismiss his prior aestheticism as far back as "Soviet Russia and the Negro": "So too, my teacher,—splendid and broadminded thought he was, yet unconsciously biased against what he felt was propaganda—thought that that gilt-washed artificiality, 'The Picture of Dorian Gray,' would outlive 'Arms and the Man' and 'John Bull's Other Island.' But inevitably as I grew older I had perforce to revise and change my mind about propaganda."[18] Still, the attitude is not wholly disingenuous, and McKay's mixed apprehension of propaganda in the late 1930s is significant because it enabled him to get a handle on the slogans that circulated in public discourse during the war. By 1939, McKay no longer felt the same need to either defend his own work as propaganda or to differentiate his poems from it. As a result, he was able to examine these phrases critically on their own terms rather than for what they might prove about the nature and function of poetry. But his complicated history also made him especially sensitive to the need for responsibility. Throughout his evolving relation to propaganda, McKay was always motivated by the belief that public language should be used with an eye toward justice. It is this principle that guided his response to the clichés of political discourse during the war, and that drew him to echo and critique, as a way of evaluating the truthfulness of rhetoric and testing it against social realities.

In deploying echo and critique, McKay focused much of his attention on nationalist rhetoric, in particular the language of shared values. Like Hughes, McKay believed that the dominant political discourse presented a false picture of American society, one that went directly against the lived reality of minorities in the United States. He also believed, as he wrote in one of his poems, that "facts remain in war and peace to flay / The falsehoods from the propaganda line."[19] Echo and critique gave him the tools to try just that, by testing the societal picture disseminated by propaganda with McKay's view of the reality on the ground.

One of the central ideas in McKay's wartime poetry is that the vision of social unity peddled by nationalist rhetoric can only deceive in a society that continues to discriminate among its citizens. For McKay, that hypocrisy was especially audible in the phrase "the American way of life." As the historian Wendy L. Wall has shown, the phrase predated World War II, but its usage exploded in the years leading up to the war and throughout the remainder of the conflict.[20] "The American way of life" was broad enough, and vague enough, that it could accommodate a variety of different political interests. Depending on the speaker, the United States' core value could be defined simplistically as representative democracy, social mobility, free market capitalism, or the middle-class lifestyle of the suburbs, to name just a few examples. Most of the time, the term was used in opposition to a real or perceived threat. During World War II, "the American way of life" was set against the dictatorship of Adolf Hitler. The journalist David Court, in an August 1940 issue of *Life* magazine, wrote:

Adolf Hitler decided that the American way of life was to inherit the earth. But he and his adopted Germans mistook for the American way of life merely its end point of efficient business management of business. He missed entirely the fact that these businessmen who looked so snappy and high-powered in their offices were in fact sons of the poor, the middle class, sometimes of immigrants, that they were little people whose energies had been released by Democracy. Hence, he missed the moral, sociological and psychological law that has made America great: the law that the best man is the one who has been allowed to make his own way.[21]

And increasingly, the other threat evoked in conjunction with the phrase was communism, a pattern that would extend further after the end of the war. In 1944, for example, a Republican candidate for the United States Senate was said by the *New York Times* to have "called upon Democratic leaders last night to support Governor Dewey for the Presidency and thus defeat the Communist threat to the American way of life."[22]

But McKay's real objection had less to do with the vagueness of the phrase, and more with the implicit assertion that "the American way of life," however it is defined, can in fact be enjoyed by all Americans equally. There was a discrepancy between nationality and "the American way of life," which could only be enjoyed by a segment of the whole society. As McKay argued in a sonnet, this deception harmed African Americans by sowing division within their communities and making them less prepared to face racism head-on.

Our boys and girls are taught in Negro schools,
That they are just like other Americans,
And grow up educated semi-fools,
And ripe for spurious words of charlatans.
The group from which they spring they all despise,
For they imagine that if not for it,
They'd have a better chance in the world to rise,
Instead of being branded as unfit!

Thus they are ready for any crazy scheme
That carries with it an offer of escape,
Although elusive as a bright sunbeam,
Or empty as the cranium of an ape.
But thus we're educated, friends and brothers,
To the American way of life—just like the others.[23]

The full force of McKay's critique stems in no small part from his careful deployment of pronouns. The poem begins with an oratorical first-person plural ("*Our* boys and girls are taught"), which is briefly allowed to sound nationalistic before its scope is redefined more narrowly as referring to African Americans at the end of the line ("in Negro schools"). This quick shift in the first line establishes the idea that it is impossible to speak in national terms—that the lives and experiences of people in the United States are dependent on race. The second line makes that idea explicit, and darkly ironic. Of course, the children are in fact Americans, but McKay argues that they are treated so differently that for all intents and purposes they might as well not be American. The line also marks a key shift in pronouns from the first- to the third-person plural "they," in reference to the children. The pronoun dominates the ten lines that follow ("they spring," "they imagine," "they are") and allows McKay to establish a critical distance toward the younger generation and how they are being miseducated. It also sets up a powerful return to the first-person plural in the couplet. "But thus we're educated, friends and brothers, / To the American way of life—just like the others." The pronoun "we" evokes the earlier promise of national unity, and the phrase "the American way of life," unfurling grandly across the final line, reinforces the effect. But that phrase, and all it promises, get swiftly undermined by a dash and a qualification: "just like the others." As a unit, the line "To the American way of life—just like the others" echoes the second, "That they are just like other Americans," with its repetition of "just" and "other." The transition from "Americans" to "the American way of life" (a stock idea that all are educated in but that not all are granted equally) also functions as a contrast, highlighting the gap between nationality and the experiences of the nation's citizens. For McKay, the falsity of "American way of life" as a concept also prevents Black people in the United States from forming a real, successful community. The poem demonstrates this by shifting repeatedly between "we" and "they." When "we" recurs in the final couplet, buttressed by an address to "friends and brothers," the pronoun is too embittered and conflicted to reassure. At most, the first-person plural has become accusatory—a reminder that the self-deception identified among the schoolchildren was also instilled in the poet's readers at some point in time.

The deep cynicism that animates this poem is a hallmark of the other sonnets that McKay published during the war. He was especially dubious about claims that the United States had made real progress in the advancement of racial equality, and lamented that this delusion was expressed in elite African American circles, too. One poem takes as example the difference in perception of the Tuskegee Normal School, a historically Black university in Alabama, in contrast to other universities attended by both Black and white students. McKay's argument culminates with the word "equality," which the latter institutions are supposed to embody, and which the poet deems hypocritical. In McKay's account, while African American "snobs" reject colleges like Tuskegee that only admit Black students on the grounds that their admissions practice "robs / The place of quality":

> the snobs declare
> That is the perfect system to defend,
> As a symbol that EQUALITY is here![24]

"EQUALITY" may appear to be granted authority by the capitalization. But the force of that term gets deflated, first, by the lowercase lettering of "here," which deprives the phrase of a climactic finish. Compare the chant-like rhythm and finality of "EQUALITY is HERE!" (which matches how the phrase would be inflected when uttered as a slogan) and "EQUALITY is here!" with its small but audible deflation right as the slogan is about to get carried off successfully. The typographical shift curbs the exclamation mark in turn, so that the punctuation becomes a sign of the snobs' inability to assert their idea with any confidence. Finally, there is also a special irony to the word "EQUALITY" standing as the only capitalized word, and thus towering over its neighbors. The discrepancy creates a visual analogy for the very real *in*equalities that the abstract word disguises.

McKay bolsters this point throughout the poem through rhyme and repetition. The sonnet is made up almost entirely of clear, full rhymes (on "snobs" and "robs," or "feet" and "elite"), the only exception being the off rhyme on "declare" and "here." The break in rhyme makes "EQUALITY is here" dissonant with the rest of the poem and suggests that there is something wrong with what the snobs "declare." Rhetoric is shown to be out of step with the reality it claims to represent faithfully. Even more complicated is the subtle repetition of "EQUALITY" and "quality" in the fourth line. The relation between these two words in McKay's thinking could be glossed a number of different ways. But the most likely reading would be to say that, behind the egalitarian claims of a word like "EQUALITY," there remains a persistent, and pernicious, concern with maintaining distinct levels of society along racial lines. For McKay, historically Black institutions that are attended by "some whites" receive praise not because they do in fact represent "equality" and put it into practice, but because the presence of white students is taken as a mark of "quality." Racial prejudice animates these institutions and the way they are perceived. By contrast, all-Black universities continue to suffer the charge of inequality when they actually present an alternative or counterpressure to white institutions.

These two poems help distinguish McKay's perspective from that of Langston Hughes, another poet who critiqued the discrepancy between the rhetoric of shared values and the lived experience of racial minorities in the United States. Hughes wished to expose the hypocrisy of white America in order to encourage political change. McKay, however, was more interested in the subtler impact of that hypocrisy on Black people in the United States. Clichés like "the American way of life" were dangerous because they had the power to convince some African Americans of an alternate reality. The hold these phrases had on the political imagination made it more difficult to push back against racial prejudice and advocate for change. But most troubling for McKay was the tendency for elite African Americans to take up these clichés in turn and, ultimately, to view "the group from which they spring" as inferior. The consequence—and, more discreetly, the function—of this rhetoric was to sow division among African Americans and damage the community building essential to political advocacy. In turn, McKay's views on the discourse of American values informed his response to the protest rhetoric in circulation, which, he believed, reflected the pressures of the dominant nationalist culture.

For McKay, the chief problem with the rhetoric of labor rights was that it too often served as a substitute for action and, in fact, prevented the kind of solidarity required for political change to occur. As always, McKay directed his ire at the intellectuals who, to his mind, were content with the status quo because it did not threaten their standing in society. One phrase that McKay returned to several times was "class struggle," a key concept from Marxist discourse. In one sonnet, he laments that even as science and religion have changed with the times,

> like a universal nursery rhyme,
> Our thinkers chant Class Struggle far and wide.[25]

The reference to "Class Struggle" as a "universal nursery rhyme" compresses several ideas into one. "Nursery rhyme" suggests that the phrase has a simplistic, childish quality, that it only expresses a "one-sided" view of life. The reference to nursery rhymes also conveys the notion of circuitousness and repetition. Like a children's song, the phrase "class struggle" is repeated widely. The problem is that the concept never translates into action or a plan for change; indeed, later he laments the absence of a "programme to end human misery." The word "universal" carries within it the idea of simplicity as well: "class struggle" gets bandied about as though it could apply everywhere, when the structure of society, and of social relations, is more complicated than this. There is the potential here for "universal" to evoke the way that race was often erased in discussions of labor rights during this time (a topic to which McKay was sensitive, as we will see later). But that idea remains a possibility in the background rather than something McKay brings to the fore and expands upon elsewhere in the poem.

Why would "class struggle" be such a simplistic notion, though? McKay's objection seems to center around the word "class," which also appears (derisively) in line 10 in reference to Karl Marx's "mystical class war," and then again in the final couplet with a rhyme on "masses": "the types we designate as masses / Have always fought the battle of the classes." In particular, the last two lines provide a window into McKay's understanding of class rhetoric. For him, the problem with phrases like "class struggle" and "the battle of the classes" is that they depict society neutrally as a conflict between various different levels which are always in tension with one another. These phrases claim to stand back and refrain from picking sides, as though the actors occupied an equal playing field. Even the nominalizations ("struggle," "battle") weaken the potential for action, so that the fight remains an abstraction. By contrast, McKay defends the term "masses," typically used with derision in reference to the working class. For him, society is best understood as an ongoing conflict between a majority of ordinary working people on the bottom, and a minority of people in power at the top. While the term "masses" may be used condescendingly, it more accurately captures the imbalance of power, and the asymmetrical relation between power and representation. It is among the working classes that the potential for action may be fulfilled: hence the attribution of the active verb "fought" to the "masses," as opposed to the nominalizations associated with intellectuals. The thinkers may talk about "the battle of the classes," but it is only the "masses" who may actually put that fight into motion.

The other problem McKay identified in the protest rhetoric of labor rights was the omission of race as a central issue in social discrimination; and this, in turn, reflected a more conscious effort among labor organizers to disregard people of color. In one poem, McKay makes this point with reference to the phrase "the labor front," writing that if he were poor and white, he would devote all of his efforts to the labor movement and chant:

The Labor Front, The Labor Front forever.[26]

That all-absorbing zeal is conveyed by repeating the phrase "The Labor Front" so that it takes over a line, capped off by the totalizing word "forever." There is the same criticism here that the rhetoric has become circuitous, self-contained, and divorced from concrete action. The second stanza breaks the repetition to uncover the pernicious reality that discourse conceals. After dismissing "the labor front" as "mere signs and symbols," he looks beyond the rhetoric at real and troubling behaviors:

White labor organized oppresses blacks,
Pushes them around in every cruel way.

Here, again, the use of active verbs and physical actions ("oppresses," "pushes them around") marks an important shift. At the same time, McKay is careful not to place the blame on the working class. The "poor white" remains a figure of sympathy, even if their allegiances and political nonaction are misguided. Instead, the phrase "white labor organized" allows McKay to blame both those in charge of organizing labor and crafting its discourse, and (more abstractly) white labor as a culture with attitudes and behaviors that may be invisible to its participants.

Here, as so often, McKay's accusations are directed at the top. In another poem, he turns his attention to "Black intellectuals" who, he says, have embraced the omission of race in labor rights discourse as a way to forget the unavoidable challenge of race in American society.

It is easy our misfortune to transfer
To blind Class Struggle, even at Heaven's gate
We shout to God his blessings to confer![27]

"Class Struggle" may pretend to be "blind," and herein lies its appeal. But the language is a "bait" and a trap. While "it is easy" admits that the intellectuals' self-deception is understandable to some extent, McKay's phrasing also carries the more biting implication that they took the easy route when they should have been more alert. With the final "we," McKay shifts his attention away from the intellectuals to Black people who suffer the consequences of this dereliction from above. They are depicted outside "Heaven," a metaphor for the world of social privilege they long to join, fruitlessly crying to receive God's blessings and enter. Yet that world is not blind to color, and neither is the discourse of "Class Struggle" that claims to help them pass the gates.

The skepticism with which McKay viewed labor rights discourse extended to the key phrases of civil rights protest rhetoric as well. Even if he did not detect in these phrases the same attempt to exclude, he did lament their futility. McKay's position was based on the belief (expressed elsewhere in his poetry, as we have seen) that rhetoric had come to stand in for, and in doing so stifle, action. The opening octave of one sonnet, published in the final year of the war, states this plainly:

> What waste of time to cry: "No Segregation!"
> When Negroes thus are in reality,
> In North and South, throughout the entire nation[28]

The slogan "No Segregation" is speedily dismissed as a mere "waste of time" when set against the reality that Black people face in America. McKay uses rhyme to establish a dismal paradox, whereby separation is revealed to be what actually unifies "the entire nation." His more specific target here is the North, the point being that even the northern states, which did not mandate segregation by law, did practice it through other means and so should be held accountable on that account. For McKay, rhetoric itself will not be sufficient to overthrowing racist laws and practices. Yet it is also a measure of McKay's despair that he cannot imagine how a different system might be realized. Earlier in the poem, he alludes to "the classic road" as the one route that white liberals can take to "defend / And follow and help," yet it is not clear what concrete steps that might entail. (Protests? Legislation?) The vagueness of McKay's image suggests he may be uncertain whether any such change is even feasible. Although he does try to maintain faith in another route, another system, McKay's skepticism has clearly slid toward cynicism. The rhyme on "reality" and "authority" has a sinister, unmovable quality, which suggests the poet has lost much of his hope.

The futility of protest language is expressed in a sonnet that robs the word "Democracy" of any direction and makes it ambiguous whether it is even uttered in protest at all. McKay laments that some African Americans treat white men as betters and "emulate them at their tricks."

> We shout Democracy around their den
> Of iniquity of jobs and politics.[29]

What makes the word "Democracy" so poignant in this context is that it remains unclear whether the term gets uttered as a demand or in celebration. The word might be asserted as if it were a lived reality for all. In this reading, African Americans are pictured talking about Democracy to emulate all those inside the "den / Of iniquity of jobs and politics," even as they are kept firmly out themselves. But the word could also be issued as a plea or petition. In this reading, African Americans demand to be let in and do not acknowledge that the realm they want to access is problematic in and of itself: a place of iniquity far removed from democratic principles. As Barbara J. Griffin notes, "McKay implies that the black man who blindly embraces the touted democratic ideal of America, a disguise for falsehood and deception, is nothing more than a duped coconspirator."[30] Without a clear goal, "Democracy" finds itself robbed of any force. It becomes an empty vessel without a real direction.

Indeed, McKay recognizes that deploying terms like "Democracy" will do nothing to curtail social inequity. Behind the accusations, there lies a lament for the inability of words to hold society accountable. At the same time, rhetorical clichés do have the power to keep those without political power under subjection. When a word like "Democracy" promises a just and equitable society, but the reality of that democracy strays far from its principles, rhetoric becomes a tool for maintaining the status quo, no matter how inequitable that social structure may be.

Perhaps the most remarkable quality of McKay's echo and critique was his recognition that clichés were not limited to people of different political sensibilities, nor to seemingly impersonal institutions like the state or the military. It is certainly easier, and more comfortable, to identify rhetorical abuse if one disagrees with the position expressed. But McKay recognized, and insisted, that cant was also evident in the discourse of individuals and organizations whose political affinities he shared. Indeed, it was all the more important to exert vigilance in these cases because it would be tempting to let politically amenable clichés slide. McKay is notable for the care he took in turning a critical eye onto his own political sensibilities, as well as those to which he was opposed.

5

ROBERT LOWELL

ON

POLITICAL SPEECHES

The period that extends from 1960 to 1975, the end point of this study, saw yet another shift in how poets responded to public speech, prompted by a broader societal change in perception. The dominant fear in this era no longer had to do with an impersonal and all-present bureaucratic state but, instead, with the expansion of executive powers, specifically in the hands of the American president. It is no surprise that "imperial presidency" became a key phrase in the 1960s, culminating in Arthur M. Schlesinger Jr.'s historical study *The Imperial Presidency* (1973). Concerns about the executive branch's rapid expansion of powers were fed by American foreign policy: the long wars against Soviet Russia and the Viet Cong, and growing public skepticism about the country's intentions. The United States had found it easier to rally in support of World War II because the cause was simple or felt so. Although both the Cold War and the Vietnam War garnered public support early on, that consensus eroded as more became concerned that America's altruism was merely imperialism in disguise.

Robert Lowell was one of the most vocal poets on the subject of the imperial presidency and American foreign policy. During the 1960s and early 1970s, Lowell adopted echo and critique to study the clichés of Cold War speech rhetoric. These stock phrases troubled Lowell because he felt that most did not make cogent political arguments, let alone present a coherent vision for society. Their goal, instead, was to shield the speaker from public criticism. By projecting equanimity, benevolence, and professionalism, oratorical clichés helped politicians evade attacks while allowing institutions to continue exercising—and abusing—power on the ground. The second danger that Lowell identified in the phrases was their potential effect on the attitudes and beliefs of ordinary citizens. To his mind, Cold War political cant fostered a narrow, simplistic view of politics and a passive relation to society. This feature extended beyond the rhetoric of the US president, which was Lowell's principal focus, to political figures who would otherwise seem to stand in opposition to the state.

Lowell traced these problems back to a change in the very practice of speechwriting. He lamented the fact that politicians did not write the statements they read to the public and that their speeches were turned out by public communication specialists tasked with avoiding the displeasure of the broadest segment of society. To Lowell, the divide between author and speaker created a high level of dishonesty. The president's words were never his own but drawn from a pool of ready-made phrases doled out for any number of situations. This concern surfaces explicitly in a later stanza of Lowell's "Waking Early Sunday Morning" (1965), where Lyndon Johnson makes an appearance:

> elated as the President
> girdled by his establishment
> this Sunday morning, free to chaff
> his own thoughts with his bear-cuffed staff,
> swimming nude, unbuttoned, sick
> of his ghost-written rhetoric![1]

The contrast between "his own thoughts" and "his ghost-written rhetoric" is instructive, as is the implicit parallel between the establishment and the speechwriters. In much the same way that the "girdle" of the president's security officers grants him the privacy needed to swim in the nude, "his ghost-written rhetoric" shields him from the public eye, so that he can be "free to chaff / his own thoughts." In other words, the ready-made language of his communication advisors keeps him from sharing, or letting slip, what he really thinks. But the protection is a devil's bargain. The final clause suggests not just wariness (he is tired of using other people's language) but also corruption and decline. The president is made sick *by* the rhetoric as much as he is sick *of* it.

In his thinking and writing on political oratory, Lowell often pitted the perceived corruption of postwar speechwriting with (what he deemed) the virtuous rhetoric of previous centuries. While the contrast betrays a streak of willful idealism in Lowell's thinking, it is worth taking these ideas seriously to better understand on what grounds he objected to the speech rhetoric of the 1960s and 1970s. The period he most admired for its oratory was nineteenth-century America. "For the Union Dead" (1960) pays tribute to William James by echoing his 1897 speech at the inauguration of the Robert Shaw Memorial on Boston Common. To Lowell, James's statement exemplified a personal, authentic form of public oratory:

> Two months after marching through Boston,
> half the regiment was dead;
> at the dedication,
> William James could almost hear the bronze Negroes breathe.[2]

In his address, William James had said: "Look at that monument and read the story—see the mingling of elements which the sculptor's genius has brought so vividly before the eye. There on foot go the dark outcasts, so true to nature that one can almost hear them breathing as they march."[3] Lowell's line lacks any indication that the image comes from another source, be it a verb or a set of quotation marks ("William James said, 'one can almost hear them'"). The omission matters because it takes what was evidently in James a rhetorical flourish—a way of further emphasizing the realism of the sculpted figures—and treats it as an impression that James truly believed he experienced. The speech is thus thought to directly reflect the feelings and opinions of the speaker. The punctuation goes even further by suggesting continuity between event and speech. The semicolon at the end of the second line marks a separation to some extent, but being less final than a period, it establishes a logical connection between the battles that took place on the field and James's response to the losses. The desire to see James's rhetoric as true to both the event itself and to his character reveals Lowell's yearning for a rhetorical ideal he can trust and aspire to now, in the midst of a Cold War and unrest at home. The poem reaches for a line of inheritance: the verisimilitude of the sculpture, matched by the honesty of both James's speech and then—or so it is hoped—this new poem.

Part of Lowell's admiration for nineteenth-century speech rhetoric, then, was its perceived honesty, as well as the direct relation between the role of writer and speaker that it evidenced. But that was not all. In a speech given to the Library of Congress for the Gettysburg Address centennial, he praised Abraham Lincoln for making his speeches akin to political actions. Predictably, Lowell pitted Lincoln against the orators of the present: "Abraham Lincoln was the last President of the United States who could genuinely use words. He and Thomas Jefferson are perhaps the only Presidents with this gift. Without his best speeches, Lincoln would have been less great as a man of action; had he not been a great statesman, he could not have written his speeches. He knew his occasion and sensed that whatever he said must have the gravity and brevity of an act of state."[4] To say that Lincoln was "the last President" to get something right is also to accuse the incumbent, pointedly, of not getting it right at all. Lowell is alluding to Lyndon Johnson, who had become head of state two months prior. His strong opinion on these two leaders leaves the rest of the historical picture muddy at best. Whereas the first sentence presents American rhetoric as a noble line cut short at Lincoln (if he was "the last President who could genuinely use words," then some or all of those who came before could do so as well), the second isolates two politicians as the sole exceptions to a general state of poverty that has always been the norm. But the ambiguities lend a certain bullheaded energy to his vision of rhetorical history. They also flesh out a particular dimension of Lowell's ideal rhetoric that will be important as we turn to the speeches of the Cold War: "He knew his occasion and sensed that whatever he said must have the gravity and brevity of an act of state." This is not quite to say that Lincoln made language and action identical, or that the president saw no distinction between the two. As Lowell indicates shortly after: "The Gettysburg Address is a symbolic and sacramental act. Its verbal quality is resonance combined with a logical, matter-of-fact, legal, prosaic brevity. It is part of the battle, a last military push that alters and adds significance to the previous military maneuvers."[5] The Gettysburg Address was "part of the battle," and it was indeed a specific, but no less important, type of "act." It brought closure and narrative shape to the military actions that had been carried out on the battlefield, and as such it had very real effects on the course of history. Importantly, though, the speech remained "symbolic and sacramental" in nature and so was of a different order than the musket shot. For Lowell, the Gettysburg Address became a rhetorical model because it completed, enlarged, and so made into history the raw facts of the Civil War. The speech may not have been a physical action, but it accomplished something that could not be performed by physical acts alone.

Compare this to Lowell's view on the speeches of the Cold War, which he believed were not acts but evasions, and which did not reveal the speaker's mind but concealed it. In his poetry, Lowell used echo and critique repeatedly to take apart the stock phrases of political oratory, exposing how they worked to shield the speaker from criticism, conceal abuses of power on the ground, and foster a passive relation to society. But like all the other poets discussed in this book, Lowell could not take comfort in the belief that he could simply set himself apart from the world of political rhetoric. He delivered a number of speeches himself against the Vietnam War and as part of Eugene McCarthy's election campaign.[6] What is more, the oratorical mode was deeply appealing to him. His poetry bears the mark of that fascination in its strong rhythms ("O Bible chopped and crucified / in hymns we hear but do not read,"), its aphoristic pronouncements ("The past changes more than the present"), and his use of the first-person plural ("We are poor passing facts").[7] Lowell was conscious of this impulse in his writing and strove to curb his oratorical style with a variety of tools, from meter and rhyme to the choice of pronouns. By echoing and critiquing the clichés of Cold War speeches, he also wished to complicate the simplistic notions of allegiance and enmity on which these speeches were built, while making it clear that he could only speak for himself, not for the country as a whole. Being a poet, his voice and perspective would remain individual, even if he felt an obligation to address the public issues of his time.

One salient example of Lowell's attention to what political stock phrases conceal and enable appears in "Pacification of Columbia," first published in the *New York Review of Books* on June 20, 1968. The poem, an unrhymed sonnet, describes the aftermath of the Columbia University riots that same year. In late April, students had barricaded themselves in five buildings on campus to protest the opening of a gymnasium they said would further ostracize the residents of Morningside Heights. (The original plans showed two separate entrances: one for Columbia affiliates, another for Harlem residents.) Police officers forced the students out of the occupied buildings on May 1, when Lowell's poem is dated.[8] The sonnet registers, and renders, the tensions that followed the reopening of the university with the description of police officers and their horses.

> horses, higher artistic types than their grooms,
> forage Broadway's median trees, as if
> nature were liberated . . . the police
> lean on the nervous, burnished hides, show they,
> at least, have learned to meet and reason together.[9]

The poet's gaze moves through the architecture and streets, taking stock of the protests' aftermath, only to land on a phrase that readers in 1968 would have recognized as one of Johnson's preferred expressions. Indeed, many of Johnson's speeches during the period, on issues ranging from labor rights to foreign policy, included just such an invitation to "reason together." He used the phrase to promote peace when the Turkish military were considering an invasion of Cyprus in 1964[10] and in the following commencement address delivered at Catholic University in 1965: "So on this Sunday morning, as you are here to bear witness, then, I would say to the people, and to the leaders, of the Communist countries, to the Soviet Union, to nations of Eastern Europe and southeast Asia; we extend to you our invitation—come, now, let us reason together. As peace knocks, our door is unlatched. Our table is set."[11] This phrase was not Johnson's own, though, but borrowed from the Book of Isaiah: "Wash you, make you clean; put away the evil of your doings from before mine eyes; cease to do evil; Learn to do well; seek judgment, relieve the oppressed, judge the fatherless, plead for the widow. Come now, and let us reason together, saith the Lord: though your sins be as scarlet, they shall be as white as snow; though they be red like crimson, they shall be as wool."[12] There is more than a glint of irony, then, in William Safire's description of "let us reason together" as "one of Lyndon Johnson's favorite phrases, stated with almost biblical sincerity."[13] This is not to say that Johnson denied his source; in fact, several of his speeches cite the Book of Isaiah explicitly: "My Daddy . . . got all us kids around the table when there was a decision to be made. He'd start off with words from Isaiah—'Come now, let us reason together.'"[14] But Johnson did repeatedly obscure the lines immediately following: "If ye be willing and obedient, ye shall eat the good of the land: But if ye refuse and rebel, ye shall be devoured with the sword: for the mouth of the Lord hath spoken it."[15] "Let us reason together," or else. Whether or not Johnson's speechwriters wished listeners to hear an implicit threat in the phrase, Lowell takes "reasoning together" as emblematic of a presidential speech rhetoric that projects benevolence while allowing violence to persist in its name. Johnson, it is important to note, never used the phrase in reference to the Columbia riots, but by associating it with the police officers, Lowell argues that the president's language provided a cover for the very abuse that they enacted in the streets.

Reading the poem with attention to the phrase's biblical origins sheds light on the pervasive threat of violence in Lowell's description of Columbia, especially in its earliest lines. The air is thick with aggressions past and potential. A "blood-warm roof-tile" might simply describes the heat of the tile, but it also evokes, darkly, the blood that was spilled when the police stormed the occupied buildings a day prior—blood that could be spilled again. The campus as a whole is a vision of sinister authority reasserted, as in "colossal classic, dungeon feudal," which evokes the danger of punishment. At the same time, Lowell's poem is clear about the concrete ways violence may be carried out. Such threats are embodied in the police officers, here described leaning against their horses on Broadway. Significantly, it is the officers who take us to the Johnson phrase, couched in a key ambiguity: "the police / lean on the nervous, burnished hides, show they, / at least, have learned to meet and reason together." The syntax gives the reader enough room to mistake the subject of the verb "show" as both "the police" and the horses, here represented by "hides," when in fact, the agents are just "the police." The officers want to show the students, pointedly, that they have learned to be reasonable and conduct themselves peacefully, unlike the protesters who may be tempted to cause further trouble. But the horses exist in a state of anxious subjugation, their hides "nervous, burnished." The uneasy peace between the men and their horses is revealed to be a lie, as any apparent consensus is forced and maintained through the implicit threat of violence. Freedom is also an illusion: "*as if* / nature were liberated.*"* Lowell reinforces this idea in the title. "Pacification," rather than "Peace," denotes something imposed. "Pacification *of*," instead of "Pacification *at*," puts emphasis on all those who were forced to comply and so made to suffer. Peace, in this moment, is the result of coercion, and the threat is manifest everywhere from national politics down to the local and the everyday (here, the policing of New York's streets).

In this context, talk of "reasoning together" becomes meaningless, but not without purpose. For Lowell, the phrase is symptomatic of a broader tendency in public communications, not just by the president but other state authorities. By urging both parties to "reason together," those in power can project an air of calm and thoughtfulness that the dissenters lack (or such is the claim). The call for dialogue becomes, paradoxically, a way to distract from the violence that institutions may inflict on the ground. At worst, it can serve as a reminder of the danger that citizens run if they oppose the state. In either case, it is certainly not intended as a step toward a real exchange of ideas. By echoing the phrase here, Lowell connects the dynamics of the New York streets at this particular moment to all levels of American politics, including foreign policy. Everywhere, the same rhetorical mechanism is at play; the response to the Columbia University protests is just one localized instance of it.

"Pacification of Columbia" reveals what Lowell believed stock phrases offered the political class: in essence, the ability to evade criticism and permit institutions to exercise power unchecked. "Fourth of July in Maine," by contrast, considers the intended effect of political cant on the public. For Lowell, the political speeches of the Cold War were dangerous because they so often peddled a narrow view of politics, and encouraged passivity and submission. The cliché that Lowell selects for evidence is the call to "resist communism": a phrase central to American political communications after World War II. It is worth looking into the history of the trope before attending to what Lowell made of it and how he attempted to push against it.

Rather than being exhorted to fight against communism, Americans in the Cold War were continually called upon to withstand its influence. This cliché was deployed in various media and so was exclusive to none, but it was especially important to political speech rhetoric. As early as 1950, Harry Truman declared to the Federal Bar Association that "we are strengthening our defenses and aiding free nations in other parts of the world so that we and they can effectively resist Communist aggression."[16] Dwight Eisenhower and John Kennedy adopted the phrase in turn during the 1950s and early 1960s.[17] No head of state, however, exploited the phrase as often as Lyndon Johnson. In a speech to the Associated Press on April 20, 1964, Johnson boasted that "we have resisted—strongly resisted—Communist efforts to extend their dominion and successfully resisted efforts to expand their power."[18] At a news conference on May 16, 1966, under the guise of a promise, he swore to the public: "Your Government, therefore, under your President, is determined to resist this aggression at the minimum cost to our people and to our allies and to the world."[19] Two months later, on July 12, he addressed "the Communists in Hanoi" while also appealing to the American public: "First, victory for your armies is impossible. You cannot drive us from South Vietnam by your force. Do not mistake our firm stand for false optimism. As long as you persist in aggression, we are going to resist."[20]

"Resistance" was attractive because it evoked national unity: all of America in it together, standing against a common foe. The language is reassuring, despite the militaristic undertones that accompany it. Johnson frames the verb "resist" in statements about what has already been achieved ("we have resisted") or will be achieved on the public's behalf ("Your Government . . . is determined to resist"). He is assuring his audience of what is now certain, not rallying them to action. Even the address to the Communists in Hanoi, which does strike militaristic overtones, gathers the American public into the pronoun "us" with no concrete indication about the actions that will be taken by the government and should be taken by the citizens. The resistance trope could flatter the audience's sense of their independence. Citizens were encouraged not to give in to an ideology that demands their submission and to be, instead, their own thinking person: an individual, even if part of a national community. To Lowell, however, this rhetoric had the quite opposite design of coddling the public into submission.

Readers of the *Atlantic* opened the March 1966 issue to find a long poem, "Fourth of July in Maine," where Lowell torques the language of resistance. The poem begins with a description of the July Fourth festivities in Castine, which serve as a springboard for talking about the political situation in America more broadly.

> Another summer! Our Independence
> Day Parade, all innocence
> of children's costumes, helps resist
> the communist and socialist.
> Five nations: Dutch, French, Englishmen,
> Indians, and we, who held Castine,
> rise from their graves in combat gear—
> world-losers elsewhere, conquerors here![21]

"Our Independence / Day Parade . . . helps resist / the communist and socialist." By rearranging the cliché, Lowell draws out a contradiction embedded within it. For a phrase about resisting ideology, notice how easily the verb "resist" itself *yields* to a rhyme on "communist and socialist." This makes the important point that appeals to defiance and independence during the Cold War came with an implicit push toward another sort of ideology to which Americans were expected to submit instead. Although the participants (children decked in costumes) may not be consciously promoting a set of political beliefs, they are nonetheless part of a broader culture in which costumes and parades in a small town in Maine serve to promote national interests against enemy powers.

John Crick argues that the poem describes "the uncomplicated politics of a contemporary Independence Day parade": the children are emblems of innocence and thus associated with the "instinctive world of animals" and the "pre-Fall Eden."[22] But the children serve less to establish the parade's innocence and more to suggest that American politics have become infantilizing and that Cold War clichés encourage a childish approach to the world. The problem becomes clear with the triple ring of "helps res*ist* / the commun*ist* and social*ist.*" The three rhymes, excessively neat to the point of being cloying, make a jingle of the resistance trope. Or, more accurately, they reveal the jingle that was there in the rhetoric to begin with. The phrase has the flash, the allure, but also the hollowness of a slogan. It oversimplifies in the same way that to align "communist" with "socialist" combines political beliefs that are distinct. Lowell doubtless has in mind the politicians who lumped the two together, or used the terms indiscriminately, as far back as the 1950s. Arthur H. Wicks, in a keynote speech at the New York Republican State Convention in September 1950, had swept both under the category of "sovietism": "In the kind of progressive, human, enlightened government that the Republican party is giving the people of New York, lies the only answer to the system for one of socialism or communism, or sovietism of any stamp or character."[23] Such talk denies the possibility of distinguishing between people who would fall under these various categories. In short, it requires that we view the political situation as children.

Granted, some aspects of this poem might seem to collude with the oratorical mode Lowell set out to critique: for example, his reliance on the strong, authoritative rhythms of the rhyming couplet. One is reminded of an interview where he was asked whether his highly publicized decision to turn down an invitation to the White House Arts Festival marked the beginning of his work as a public poet. Lowell responded by speaking of poetic form: "Perhaps the meter I chose, Marvell's eight-line stanza, mattered more. It hummed in my mind summer till fall. It's possible to have a good meter yet bad intention or vice versa—*vers de société,* or gauche sprawl. All summer long, as I say, the steady, hypnotic couplet beat followed me like a dog."[24] In a poem that takes the jingoistic march of a July Fourth parade as representative of a broader problem in American politics, the use of a "steady, hypnotic beat" would appear to bring the poet alarmingly close to the sort of militaristic pageantry he wished to knock. The poem itself tells a different story, though. Although Lowell was drawn to the Marvellian line for its leanness and clarity, the couplets do not lock words into rhyme so much as pull them into jarring association. A third of the rhymes are near-rhymes or eye rhymes (twenty-three out of sixty-eight total), and even those that qualify as full rhymes land at a right angle from each other, so that each pair works against itself. Consider the first stanza's final couplet, in which the costumed fighters are said to

> rise from their graves in combat gear—
> world-losers elsewhere, conquerors here!

The stanza's conclusion is made anticlimactic halfway through the final line. The disparity between America's self-image ("conquerors here!") and its true position abroad ("world-losers elsewhere")—not to mention the near-rhyme on "here" and "elsewhere" that underlines the disparity—cancels out whatever dramatic peak might have been struck by the couplet's full rhyme on "gear" and "here." The stanza's opening lines perform similar work in an even more complex fashion:

> Another summer! Our Independence
> Day Parade, all innocence
> of children's costumes

Capitalized "Independence" is set against the smallness, and fragility, of a lowercase "innocence," even as the two are said to be in cahoots this Fourth of July. The tendency, when reading couplets, to foreground the rhymes with a pause and an emphasis gets swept up by the pull of each enjambment ("Our Independence / Day Parade," "innocence / of children's costumes"). There is also the jolting effect of stress patterns that come very close to matching but do not quite correspond: "*In* | de | *pen* | dence" versus "*all* | *in* | no | cence." The near-rhyme reflects on the subordination of innocence to nationalism, even as it compels us to think more complicatedly about the relation between these two states of being: whether innocence can actually be compatible with independence, whether it is possible to experience either of these states without the rhetorical baggage that accompanies them, and so on.

In short, the poem fights its own desire for a "steady, hypnotic beat" that would direct the reader through a sequence of orderly pairs. Instead, it associates discrete elements only to make the relation between them unsettled and uncertain. Lowell keeps the reader on the alert with a metrical pattern that shifts from couplet to couplet. This trick is accompanied by other strategies to counter both the infantilizing simplicities of Cold War rhetoric and the risk (which the poet runs) of falling into those rhetorical patterns in turn. For instance, the speaker takes apart the first-person plural used so authoritatively in "*Our* Independence / Day Parade." The first-person plural is the basis of much public oratory: a way for the speaker to include a broader national community in their address or to include themselves in the community they are addressing and so claim a partnership with them. "We" and "our" were common currency in presidential speeches that called the public to resist communism ("we have resisted," "we are going to resist"). Lowell was troubled by the simplicity of that usage, and "Fourth of July in Maine" shows him splitting the pronoun into a host of different constituents. The second half of the first stanza, again:

> Five nations: Dutch, French, Englishmen,
> Indians, and we, who held Castine,
> rise from their graves in combat gear—
> world-losers elsewhere, conquerors here!

The cohesion suggested by the opening "our" finds itself divided into "Five nations: Dutch, French, Englishmen, / Indians, and we." The first-person plural recurs, but its reach is far less certain than at the beginning of the stanza. Who does the pronoun include or exclude at this juncture of the poem? The question is complicated by the history of Castine and its surroundings: a disputed territory for a large part of colonial American history, between the French to the north, the English to the south, the Abnaki who had originally inhabited the area, and, to a lesser extent, the Dutch.[25] During the War of Independence, the British sought to reclaim the area and succeeded until a peace settlement was signed in 1783.[26] Lowell's first-person plural could be said to pit American revolutionaries against rival colonists, imperial powers, and indigenous populations, in which case the "we" appears rather diminutively and weakly at the end of the sequence. Read so, the stanza continues Lowell's mockery of what

Cold War rhetoric leaves out or distorts, like the historical fact that the revolutionaries did not quite hold Castine for the duration of the war.

But it is also important to the poem that many revolutionaries were of English, French, and Dutch descent, so that it becomes hard to draw a clear line between friend and foe. Read with a shift in emphasis, the sequence of nations can be interpreted as a picture of the five populations who, by squabbling and settling and resettling, collectively held Castine and now make up its past: the history of Castine as the history of five nations. This takes the poem beyond the bounds of ironic imitation. Lowell does not quite argue that American identity is pluralistic, or a single identity made of very many differences (*e pluribus unum*), which itself has a long history in American rhetoric. Rather the poem asserts that the United States is made up of many collaborating-conflicting nations, and that its history cannot be separated from the history of the world. America in 1965 is the result of what many nations—both friends and foes—have enacted.

In countering reductive uses of the first-person plural by the political establishment, Lowell criticizes the impoverishment of a "we" that does not recognize its own plurality and believes it can stand, and has stood, alone. Much of Cold War rhetoric troubled Lowell precisely because it fostered submission and pushed citizens to subsume their identity within a limited, nationalist vision. Here he uses a variety of techniques to complicate that vision while also setting clear limits to the scope and authority of his own eloquence.

Though little may seem to unite Lowell and Claude McKay, both poets did share the belief that they had a responsibility to critique stock phrases of varied political viewpoints, including those to which they were personally agreeable. A conscientious objector during World War II and a participant in several protests against the Vietnam War, Lowell was profoundly suspicious of American military interventions abroad. Yet his poetry also turns a critical eye to the stock phrases used to protest the conflicts. Because he generally tended to agree with the political cause, Lowell sought other ways to complicate or refine the stock phrases of protest rhetoric.

Rather than contesting the central tenet of these phrases (namely, that American military interventions do more harm than good), he worked to mitigate their tendency to reinforce alliances and animosities—the very same impulse that disturbed him in presidential speech rhetoric.

The most moving example of this occurs in "Waking Early Sunday Morning." In the final stanza, Lowell takes up a distant, cosmic perspective on the United States, calling on his readers to "Pity the planet." He lands on a common phrase of the Vietnam War era, lamenting that America is condemned

> until the end of time
> to police the earth, a ghost
> orbiting forever lost
> in our monotonous sublime.[27]

Frank Bidart and David Gewanter attribute the phrase "police the earth" to journalism, specifically Walter Lippmann's opinion pieces for *Newsweek:* "Our official doctrine is that we must be prepared to police the world against aggression."[28] Yet the history of this phrase stretches much further back. Benjamin Harrison made use of it six years after his presidency, in an 1899 speech to the American Chamber of Commerce in Paris: "The United States has not set eyes upon distant possessions. America has never failed either in Greece, Armenia, or South America, to make it known that she reprobated cruelty and persecution, but she has not felt that she has a commission to police the world."[29] The phrase later became a slogan of American isolationism, used by Hiram Johnson to oppose the League of Nations after World War I ("In a word, Mr. President, this league means that American boys shall police the world");[30] by Herbert Hoover to argue against the nation's entry into World War II ("How are we going to secure that liberty and freedom and democracy be accepted by those races whose whole racial instincts rebel against it? Are we going to police the world?");[31] and by numerous critics of the Vietnam War, most notably Paul Potter, the president of Students for a Democratic Society, in front of fifteen thousand people on the grounds of the Washington Monument:

What kind of system is it that justifies the United States or any country seizing the destinies of the Vietnamese people and using them callously for its own purpose? What kind of system is it that disenfranchises people in the South, leaves millions upon millions of people throughout the country impoverished and excluded from the mainstream and promise of American society, that creates faceless and terrible bureaucracies and makes those the place where people spend their lives and do their work, that consistently puts material values before human values—and still persists in calling itself free and still persists in finding itself fit to police the world?[32]

Potter delivered this speech at the first national protest against American foreign policy in Vietnam, on April 17, 1965.[33] Lowell, who likely had Potter in mind when he wrote "Waking Early Sunday Morning," published his poem in the *New York Review of Books* less than four months later on August 5, 1965.

Although his position on the Vietnam War would seem to overlap with the pacifist sentiment expressed in the phrase "police the earth," Lowell avoids simply lending his support. For like other clichés that he objected to on ideological grounds, this particular slogan aims to divide as much as persuade, and it also simplifies. Lowell complicates the phrase by shifting its tenor and intent. The image of America "policing the earth" becomes mournful rather than accusatory, and indeed the poet frames the expression within a call for "pity." This effect is extended by a shift in proportion. Political figures used the phrase "police the earth" to depict the monstrosity of America as the world's superpower: the United States grown to terrible size, marching across the globe and extending its military might. Lowell, by contrast, portrays America as a mere diminutive "ghost," orbiting the planet yet obviously and pathetically unable to carry out any meaningful designs. The effect is deepened, as well, by the pitiful implications of what follows. "A ghost / orbiting forever lost": it is unclear if "forever" qualifies the verb "orbiting" or the adjective "lost," and although neither would radically change the meaning of the lines, the syntactical ambiguity does cause "forever" to hover tragically, lost in the grammar of the sentence. The central idea here is that America is losing itself by engaging in foreign conflicts. The loss may be greater on the other side, but the United States will not escape unharmed from its expansion of power.

In short, Lowell echoes a phrase that was used simply to attack and turns it into a bid for sympathy. By doing so, he counters, at least within the scope of this poem, the tendency of political stock phrases to assert simple alliances and enmities. At the same time, he sets firm limits on his own pretenses as a political speaker. While the tone and rhythm of the stanza may sound oratorical, Lowell is careful not to present his poem as a solution to the problems that he identified in political discourse. Curiously, several critics have read the poem's ending as victorious. William Doreski, for instance, writes: "The argument seems to be that . . . self-obsession must give way to empathy—even empathy with the president—to induce the proper note of unsententious grief."[34] Ian Hamilton, in a more moderate vein, says that "because of his distrust of easy rhetoric [Lowell] finally—indeed triumphantly—achieves a rhetoric that we can trust; a rhetoric of painful and profound 'unease.'"[35] Yet this, too, is likely claiming too much, for Lowell remains wary about his relation to the sphere of public oratory until the very end. This is evident in the way his perspective evolves over the course of the stanza. At first, the opening couplet, "Pity the planet, all joy gone / from this sweet volcanic cone," appears (troublingly) to view the planet from a superior, perhaps even divine perspective. "*This* volcanic cone" implies a sweeping gesture at the earth laid out before him, and the particular brand of feeling advocated is telling: not sympathy, nor even empathy, but pity. The grandness of the tone further supports this impression of a poet somehow greater than, and separate from, the planet he exhorts us to pity. Lowell is part of the planet himself, of course, but the first two lines do not seem willing to acknowledge the fact. After these two lines, however, he lowers his position to counteract the pretensions of his opening command. A first-person plural appears, as in "Fourth of July in Maine," but this time Lowell is even less certain how he should define its reach. "Peace to our children / when they fall in small war on the heels of small / war": the children of America, or of the planet as a whole? By the time we have arrived at the last four lines, and the image of America "policing the earth" in particular, it has become impossible to tell from what vantage point Lowell is viewing this imagined scene: on earth, looking up at the orbiting ghost, or up in the sky, watching the planet from afar.

The poem's grim conclusion can be understood as a capitulation to the insoluble problem of rhetoric. The line "in our monotonous sublime"—itself monotonous with its sequence of oratorical *o*'s—is a lament for the tiresome routine of public rhetoric as much as it is a commentary on the centrality of war to American politics. "Waking Early Sunday Morning" ends on a note of profound skepticism as to the poet's ability to offer a reliable alternative to the politician. If the poem succeeds as a poem, it is because Lowell knew to concede its limitations. He is as alien from political oratory as he is from the realm of policymaking where political decisions are made. It was important to him, however, that his poem stand as a failed rhetorical performance and thus testify to the problems of public rhetoric. "Waking Early Sunday Morning" resolves nothing, and knows it cannot, but it does bring our attention to the distinctive features of political oratory.

Lowell's poetry laments the corruption of American political oratory and its transformation into an evasive "ghost-written rhetoric" built on ready-made phrases, and it hears in those phrases a troubling attempt to skirt responsibility and infantilize the public. Yet his critique of political rhetoric was also energized and complicated by his attraction to the grandeur of oratorical writing. Granted, he recognized that poets and politicians address different audiences: a literary readership on the one hand (whoever happens to pick up the poem and give it their attention) and the nation as a whole on the other (though not everyone may tune in, a political speech is presumably written to be heard by all). Yet he also knew that the poet and politician faced similar risks: the arrogance of claiming too much and speaking too readily for others. For Lowell, who wanted to be a truly public writer, these poems enabled him to consider how he might play that role without succumbing to the problems he witnessed in the political realm.

6

JOSEPHINE MILES
ON
BUSINESS TALK

Whereas Robert Lowell, througout his career, focused his echo and critique on presidential speech rhetoric, Josephine Miles began her career in the late 1930s examining a variety of discourses, from bureaucratese to academese. By the mid-1960s, however, she had narrowed her attention onto what seemed to her the most important phenomenon in public language: the infiltration of business talk into every area of civic life. In this regard, she reflected a broader social concern about the spread of business clichés in public discourse, especially in the political sphere. Indeed, for many intellectuals, more and more real political power was to be found not in the hands of the American president and other elected officials, but in the CEOs of international corporations. Business interests increasingly determined public policy, and political discourse bore the mark of this influence. It is for these insights that Miles's poetry holds particular interest in the history of echo and critique, for she was one of the first poets to examine this development in public speech extensively across multiple poems.

Curiously, Miles was praised early on for not allowing any specialized discourse to encroach upon her verse. Jessica Nelson North, writing in 1935, praised Miles for keeping the language of poetry a distinct province: "Philosophy, social theories, propaganda, all have their place in prose, but not in poetry. Load any poem with a heavy cargo of purpose and it goes down to the bottom with no hope of salvation."[1] Forty years later, Helen Vendler commended Miles in similar terms, saying that she had found a way to address current events without resorting to combative language: "There is a need for more poems of this sort, poems, so to speak, of the day's news, now largely a preserve of interested propagandists."[2] But Miles believed in a far more complex interplay between poetry and public speech than her critics allowed. For one, she held that social practice shaped poetry by virtue of its medium. In *The Continuity of Poetic Language* (1965), an ambitious study of English language poetry from the 1540s to the 1940s, she contended:

> To describe the common materials of language through which poets work is to describe at once the limitations and the potentialities of their medium. The language which the makers speak is not amorphous and not by any means susceptible of free improvisation. Its sounds and sentence structures, and the references and associations of its words, are well set for poets as for everyone else by social situation in time and place. . . . Among the arts, in fact, literature may be distinguished by this very intense conditioning of its medium. The tones of the musician, the stones of the sculptor, are full of their character at the outset, but that character has not been so strongly socialized, so loaded with meaningful and valuable forms and associations, as has the language which the man of letters accepts to work with. Sentences and words cannot be neutral, nor can, for the poet specifically, the sounds and measures of sentences and words.[3]

To write poetry is to wade into a medium riddled with associations, references, and conventions; that much cannot be avoided and constitutes one of the form's "limitation." But one potentiality would be to then play with that linguistic freight, to examine it and critique it.

Over the past twenty years, critics have started paying attention to the dynamic relationship Miles envisioned between poetry and the social matrix of which it is a part. Zofia Burr has written that Miles feels "disinclined to view poetic language as a special object removed from the ordinary occasions of language use."[4] Erik Muller has also said that she "used common language in her own poetry, considering that an era gives a voice to the poet rather than the poet to an era."[5] Still, it is worth drawing a distinction between everyday speech used in conversation between family, friends, and fellow citizens, and the more specialized discourse that citizens in their public lives occasionally use and more often confront. Miles associated everyday speech with vitality. She made this point in an interview with Naomi Clark:

> Sometimes when I hear people say something, hear spoken language or see language written, there's a kind of special energy to it which makes me feel that's something I ought to try to keep hold of. Soon, or maybe a long time after, I try to shake it up a bit as a way of keeping it. There's a source of vitality from people. The sense of meaning in what's being said—that's probably where I contribute to something.[6]

Reframing and repurposing bits of ordinary speech in poetry enabled her to preserve its liveliness, so that a reader could experience both the pleasure of recognition (upon encountering a phrase that has been heard before) and the surprise of seeing it transformed. Her response to specialized discourses like business talk reveals a different attitude. For Miles, these speech genres represent a dead language that is out of touch with life. Granted, she took pleasure in reframing and repurposing phrases from these discourses, and she clearly expected her readers to share both the pleasure of recognition and the shock of transformation. But the poet's aim is not to celebrate the vitality of this language but to expose its deadness.

Miles critiqued an impressive variety of public discourses throughout her writing life, from bureaucratese to the specialized language of journalism and real estate. For Miles, the clichés that populate these various speech genres pose a danger not only because they are devoid of meaning but more importantly because they are divorced from lived experience.

They divorce both speaker and listener from the vitality of ordinary speech that would otherwise help lend shape to their lived experience. Miles's background as a scholar informed her typological approach to the material. While teaching at the University of California, Berkeley, she published two books, *Major Adjectives in English Poetry* (1946) and *The Continuity of Poetic Language* (1951), examining the features that defined each era of English poetry. She applied the same methodical approach to the discourses that she echoed and critiqued. At the same time, her experience working in academia made her conscious of the clichés populating her own professional discourse, *academese.* She could not assume that cant was something other people used elsewhere, and that awareness led her, like many other poets who engaged in echo and critique, to turn a critical eye inward as well as outward.

One example of Miles's self-critical approach can be found in "Maxim," from *Neighbors and Constellations* (1960). There the poet playfully applies clichés of academese to the kitschy display of a Rose Bowl Parade:

It is said that certain orientational concepts of an ontological sort
Such as despair, sin, salvation, loneliness
Derive a certain richness from experience.

I noticed today at the Rose Bowl Parade
In the Romeo and Juliet float representing Wonder Bread,
How lonely Romeo shirtsleeved

In the frosty morning air looked, saluting
(1) the balcony made of thousands of blossoms of pink winter stock,
And (2) the curbstone crowd.

This won the sweepstakes prize, yet Juliet
Smiled in despair in the frosty morning air,
Receiving her certain richness from experience.[7]

The first stanza lurches between academic discourse and ordinary speech in order to emphasize the abstract nature of academese. The opening line is dominated by philosophical terminology that does not state its meaning plainly. What, for example, is an "orientational concept"? The phrase is further cushioned by "certain": a mundane word that often appears in academic writing in order to give the impression of a more nuanced argument, without doing the work of drawing distinctions. Here, for instance, what concepts would be excluded from the list? Empty stylistic flourishes reappear at the end of the line when the specialized term "ontological" is needlessly padded into "of an ontological sort." The second line breaks that jargon with a refreshing sequence of plain words, denoting either emotions or religious ideas: "despair, sin, salvation, loneliness." The pretentions of the opening line cannot stand up to the directness of this list; they are shown to be empty and purposeless by contrast. When the third line returns to the formality, restraint, and vagueness of academese with "Derive *a certain richness from experience,*" that specialized discourse seems comically out of touch with what real despair and loneliness feel like.

The stanzas that follow take this opening thesis and apply it to a specific instance. The joke here lies in the selection of a Rose Bowl Parade as the poet's case study. The poem is now quite far from the academic realm and has entered the world of commerce and popular entertainment. Miles makes a quick jab at academic prose with the seemingly rigorous—but pointless—use of numbers to delineate a list. But her real focus is on the clash between the abstract language of academic writing and the scene to which it is applied. The artifice of the Rose Bowl Parade serves a double function: it brings out the artifice of academese by association, and also underlines the reality of the emotions that the actors feel, even if they cannot express them openly, as it would break the illusion of their performance. *How lonely Romeo looked, Juliet smiles in despair.* When "a certain richness of experience" resurfaces to describe Juliet, the phrase now seems comically out of touch with what the actors feel. Academese fails because it cannot capture the ideas and emotions it claims to describe. Miles's use of Romeo and Juliet evokes Lionel Trilling's attack on abstract language in "The Meaning of a Literary Idea" (1949), which she may have had in mind: "A specter haunts our culture—it is that people will eventually be unable to say, 'They fell in love and married,' let alone understand the language of *Romeo and Juliet,* but will as a matter of course say, 'Their libidinal impulses being reciprocal, they activated their individual erotic drives and integrated them within the same frame of reference.' Now this is not the language of abstract thought or of any kind of thought. It is the language of non-thought."[8] To which Miles would likely add: the language of non-feeling.

The mid-1960s witnessed a shift in her use of echo and critique, however. Starting with the book *Civil Poems* (1966), and continuing in *Kinds of Affection* (1967) and *Fields of Learning* (1968), Miles refocused her attention on business speak, driven by the belief that the language of economics and advertising had permeated every genre of public discourse, most strikingly in politics. She was not alone in this conjecture. The philosopher and sociologist Herbert Marcuse, writing in 1964, came to a similar diagnosis on the uneasy cooperation of business and politics:

If the language of politics tends to become that of advertising, thereby bridging the gap between two formerly different realms of society, then this tendency seems to express the degree to which domination and administration have ceased to be a separate and independent function in the technological society. This does not mean that the power of the professional politicians has decreased. The contrary is the case. The more global the challenge they build up in order to meet it, the more normal the vicinity of total destruction, the greater their freedom from effective popular sovereignty. But their domination has been incorporated into the daily performances and relaxation of the citizens, and the "symbols" of politics are also those of business, commerce, and fun.[9]

For Marcuse, the problem with muddling politics and advertising is that it disguises the politician's will to dominate, by dressing it up in the language of "business, commerce, and fun." This concern was voiced by many other public figures in the decades that followed, including journalists, linguists, historians, and political scientists, and, indeed, that anxiety is still with us today. What follows are just a few examples. In 1973, the linguist Mario Pei lamented that "the world of commercial advertising" had come to dominate political advocacy: "Movements of all kinds (whether officially organized, like political parties; half-organized, like civil rights movements, antidefamation leagues, women's liberation groups; utterly disorganized, like the Youth Culture) reek of the language of public relations, a language designed to enhance a given cause in the eyes of the would-be indifferent, and force him to become 'involved' and bestir himself on behalf of that cause."[10] In 1981, Hugh Rawson criticized the use of business speak as political euphemisms—a phenomenon which served to make entire industries out of war, politics, and justice.

> Here, too, are our great industries: the prison business, where solitary confinement cells are disguised as *adjustment centers, quiet cells,* or *seclusion;* the atomic power business, where nuclear accidents become *core rearrangements* or simply *events;* the death business, where *remains* (not bodies) are *interred* (not buried) in *caskets* (not coffins); and finally, of murder on its largest scale, where people are put into *protective custody* (imprisonment) in *concentration camps* (prison camps) as a first step toward achieving the *Final Solution* (genocide).[11]

In 1993, John Barry described "an infusion of businessbabble into the language: *bottom line, greenmail, leveraged,*" starting in the 1980s, which subsequently morphed into the "computerese" of technology companies. This lingo, too, aimed to sell both products and ways of relating to those items, as in the example of *"personal computer"*: "*Personal computer* was a friendly-sounding alternative to the technical term *microcomputer.* The friendly phrase added a personal touch to an industry noted for its impersonal nature. Initially, the term suggested an intimate, one-on-one relationship between user and machine—no big machine in a back room somewhere; no timesharing, in which users had to wait their turn to exploit a small portion of a minicomputer's resources. The personal computer was all the user's (an interface right in your face)."[12] In 2005, Don Watson argued that the decay which Orwell had identified in political language was now evident in business, and "the use of business models in places that were never businesses":

> Libraries, galleries and museums, banks and welfare agencies now parrot it. The public sector spouts it as loudly as the private does. It is the language of all levels of government, including the very local. Your local library is now apt to speak of *focusing on the delivery of*

outputs and matching decisions to *strategic initiatives.* Almost invariably these *strategic initiatives* are *key* strategic initiatives. In this language, schools, bank branches, and libraries are closed down. In an education curriculum or the *mission statement* of an international fast food chain you will hear the same phrases. In many Australian schools eleven-year-olds are asked to write mission statements that define their key personal values and goals. Military leaders while actually conducting wars sound like marketing gurus, and politicians sound like both of them. If one day in the finance pages you encounter *critical deliverables,* do not be surprised if it turns up the next day when you're listening to the football game. The public language has all these variants, and all of them are infected, if not dead. It is the gray death of the globalized world.[13]

The fact that Miles was one of the first poets to examine this phenomenon in depth across multiple poems is significant, making her an important figure in the history of echo and critique.

It is surprising, then, that she chose to include so little of *Civil Poems* or *Fields of Learning* in her *Collected Poems* (1983): only three and four poems, respectively, and none that echo and critique corporate language. Lisa Steinman has put forward one hypothesis. She praises "Miles' ability to treat topical subjects without abandoning the nuances and, more, the ethical questioning and self-questioning, characteristic of her early work," but wonders how many would read these poems and recognize "the careful modulation and honesty in such poetry, instead of responding to (or reacting against) the political rhetoric such poems invoke in order to resist."[14] Miles herself has never spoken about the exclusion of key political poems from the mid- to late 1960s. It seems likely that she had more faith in her readers than this. Perhaps she saw them as too closely tied to the sociopolitical context she was responding to and so felt that they lost their relevance with time. Or perhaps she simply ceased finding much merit in them. But these poems are worth turning back to, both because they are important to the history of echo and critique and because their obscurity has led them to be greatly underappreciated.

Before delving into these poems, it is worth noting that Miles's approach might seem closer to pastiche than what I call echo and critique.

Unlike most of the poems discussed previously, which zero in on a single phrase, Miles typically takes up a variety of phrases from a chosen discourse. Still, unlike the work of Kenneth Goldsmith (to borrow my example from the introduction), her peculiar juxtaposition still generates specific criticisms about individual clichés—sometimes through rhyme, tone, structure, or imagery in a phrase's surrounding context, other times by playing clichés off one another—rather than presenting them with an air of neutrality. In sum, her intention and attitude to public discourse remains the same, but her scope has widened to encompass both more phrases and to consider more directly the broader types of discourse that these individual phrases represent.

Miles first developed her insights about the expansion of business talk in *Civil Poems* (1966). One poem in this collection, "Freedoms," plays on Franklin D. Roosevelt's 1941 State of the Union address, in which he laid out "four freedoms" that everyone in the world should enjoy (freedom of speech, freedom of worship, freedom from want, and freedom from fear). Miles imagines how the phrase might be reappropriated to advertise a senior living community and its amenities. This leads to a comedy of contrasts, between the momentous crisis of World War II and the mundanity of life after retirement, though Miles exploits the gap to make a serious point. The unusual application of business talk reveals the extent to which corporate language has taken over public life, and politics has failed. Businesses have rushed in to meet the needs that should be fulfilled by elected officials.

Ten new freedoms
In Mossmore Senior City.
For the young in heart at sixty,
Ten new ways to be free.

To be free first from boredom,
Then from appliance maintenance,
Then from noise and nuisance
And various medical fees.

Then free from the chores of gardening,
From loneliness, house-cleaning,
From transportation worries
And tiresome shopping needs.

And more! Are there more freedoms?
Freedom from old clamors
In towns called Philadelphia:
From reasons to be free.[15]

Roosevelt's vatic declaration ("In the future days, which we seek to make secure, we look forward to a world founded upon four essential human freedoms")[16] turns into a bright, inviting advertisement: "Ten new freedoms." The tendency of advertising lingo toward excess gets mocked by the inflation of *four* to *ten,* as well as by the belated and unsubstantiated promise of the final stanza: "And more!" The poem as a whole is riddled with phrases that are either clichés in and of themselves or that swirl around that category. These range from the stock phrases of bureaucratic paperwork (like "appliance maintenance," "medical fees") to the clichés of everyday conversation (the platitude of being "young in heart"). Together, the phrases paint a gray picture of life weighed down by mundanity. Mossmore Senior City promises to liberate its citizens (or clients?) from various nuisances, from housecleaning to "transportation worries," but amid the litany of routine complaints, "loneliness" stands out and prompts skepticism. After all, "loneliness" is the one thing that Mossmore Senior City cannot simply resolve. For Miles, a deep emotional vacuum lies beneath the surface of everyday middle-class life. Material comforts will never fill it, and indeed they might accentuate the problem.

Miles is interested here in what happens to "freedom" when that political concept becomes a product that is then advertised and sold. The most obvious consequence is that the idea finds itself impoverished. Freedom of speech, freedom of worship, freedom from fear do not feature anywhere in the poem. It would be tempting to view Mossmore Senior City as a place that reduces liberty to freedom from want, but the poem's emphasis is less on an abundance of objects, furniture, or even services, and more on the lack of minor annoyances. As a result, the clients never have to work to overcome or avoid those nuisances. The poem might be understood as a commentary on the plush comforts of senior living communities, but Miles clearly sees Mossmore Senior City as a microcosm of consumerist society more broadly. The idea here is that real freedom requires effort. Consumerist society seems to offer an abundance of choices, but actually promises to unburden us from having to work or make more difficult choices on our own. For Miles, the will to be free *of* freedom is the secret desire underlying contemporary society, which advertising exploits. But to her mind, this is not a burden we should avoid.

The influence of business talk in every area of public discourse had important consequences for politics, and foreign policy in particular. During an era of "American intervention," the language of war and advertising became curiously intertwined. The goal was to soften the militaristic nature of the United States' actions abroad by speaking innocuously of "aid." The audience was made up not only of the people on the other side of those actions but also the citizens of the United States who needed to be persuaded that America's new role in the world was fundamentally good. Miles addresses this problem in the poem "Necessities":

> You do not want the vote? We will help you win it.
> You tire of foreign aid? Let us aid your tiredness.
> You sicken at white faces over black rifles?
> Whiten your own; there are more where these came from.
>
> Such is the economy of abundance that it can furnish
> Infinite amounts of what nobody asks for,
> And at no great sacrifice, except of principle,
> Escalate surfeit to a disease like death.[17]

Much like in Auden's "The Unknown Citizen," the speaker evokes the impersonality of government authorities, overlaid with the poet's ironic perspective. The first stanza works through a series of questions and answers yet tellingly never in the voice of those whose countries are being invaded; they remain silent throughout. Instead, the government parrots their concerns and claims to provide reassurance by reversing their terms and going against their intentions. In "You tire of foreign aid?" the word "aid" supplies the main verb for "Let us aid your tiredness," thus emptying it of meaning. After all, the United States cannot truly speak of "aid" if its actions do not help those on the other side. Miles shows America imposing on other nations what they do not want, be it the vote or, in a more sinister vein, the appearance of "white faces over black rifles." As the stanza grinds on, the speaker's attitude becomes more bullyish. The government goes from assuring the people that they will "help," to pleading that they submit to America's actions ("let us"), to issuing orders ("Whiten your own") with cold indifference ("there are more where these came from"). For Miles, the talk of "aid" functions as a euphemism to conceal imperialistic designs.

In the second stanza, Miles connects military interventions abroad to capitalism through the phrase "economy of abundance." The idea is that both impose a vast supply of "what nobody asks for," and for the benefit of only a few. Instead of cereal and washing machines, military intervention supplies "infinite amounts" of soldiers and, with them, American social, cultural, and political habits. "There are more where these came from," in reference to "white faces," has about it the whiff of advertising which the second stanza draws out in retrospect. Miles does not simply draw a parallel between two systems based on common features; rather, she argues that America's military actions depend on capitalism and are a part of it, delivering an endless supply of soldiers and weaponry.

The final line brings to a head the odd partnership of war and capitalism. "Escalate surfeit," an ungainly combination, brings together the linguistic realms of the military ("escalate") and the economic ("surfeit"). The word "to" is hard to parse in this context and makes the grammar of the sentence difficult to understand. The intended meaning appears to be that the excess produced by capitalism, and war under capitalism, will only increase to the point of death. Military intervention will continue to lay countless soldiers and civilians low, and those deaths will simply become a part of war's "abundance." Similarly, in America, an endless supply of things to buy will not save people from death. In fact, capitalism may quicken death by sacrificing the health of communities and the environment for profit. (Poems in *Kinds of Affection* [1967], for example, describe the aquatic life of the San Francisco Bay being choked out of existence to make way for "a bowling alley, / A car park and golf course.")[18] Though this may be the clearest condemnation of American foreign policy in the poem, Miles does not drop her persona entirely. To talk about death as a "disease" is a sign that the speaker fails to recognize its inevitability; death is not something to be cured. At the same time, the word evokes the inhuman machinery of war and economics that always goes on beyond human mortality. How much greater the abundance would be, if goods or buyers never had to be sacrificed.

In *Kinds of Affection* (1967), Miles continued to examine the vast influence of corporate lingo in public life, though by using a different approach. As in "Maxim," she stressed the problems of business clichés by setting individual phrases within a context that appears alien to them. This time, however, the context is absurd, evoking the world of jokes, folktales, and children's stories. The contrast both reveals the absurdity of the clichés by association, and emphasizes the seriousness of their implications by contrast.

One poem reflects, and mocks, the importance of the entrepreneur in the business world by imagining him as a chicken. The absurdist touch diminishes the entrepreneur's status (and hints that he is not as important as he thinks), but it also makes his influence on the surrounding cityscape all the more shocking. For the entrepreneur does have power, even if his ego far outstrips his reach.

The entrepreneur chicken shed his tail feathers, surplus
Fat, his comb, wing weight, down to a mere
Shadow, like a Graves bird ready to sing.
For him every morning
Paradise Merchant Mart reopened its doors
With regular fire sales, Shoe Parlor
Blackened its aroma, Professional
Building ran its elevators up and down
So fast that pulled teeth turned up in other mouths.

Activity. The tax base broadened in the sunlight
As gradually sun spreads wider after coffee.
It was a busy world on that side of the road,

For which the entrepreneur chicken was in his able
Way responsible.
At noon, loans, mortgages, personal interest,
At night notarized after-images, as if by sundown
The elevator had turned to moving sidewise
Frames and phrases to be read and reread.[19]

To imagine a chicken as an entrepreneur may be absurd, yet this chicken is depicted quite seriously as the center of the business world, holding outsized influence on what surrounds him. The whole economy works "for" him and in his service. The chicken's ever-expanding control finds its most potent expression in the spread of business language across these two stanzas. Body fat is referred to, slightingly, as "surplus." The sun's scope is associated with the expansion of the "tax base." (The logic seems to be that stores operate mostly during the day, so the "tax base" increases any time the sun is out.) The landscape is dominated not only by "fire sales" and "Professional Buildings" but also by heaps of bureaucratic paperwork: "loans, mortgages, personal interest." The entrepreneur does not see a community, nor a city, nor even a society, but an economy, in which activity and relations are defined only by financial transactions. Indeed, there is a good reason why Miles isolates "Activity" emphatically at the start of the second stanza. The word is not solely or inherently economic, but its specialized use here, in reference to the exchange of money, goods, and services, reflects what Erik Muller has called "the narrow interests of the profit taker."[20] For the entrepreneur, activity only has value—and can only be recognized as such—if it is of the kind that can be monetized.

After lamenting the entrepreneur's power, Miles uses the image of the chicken to put the entrepreneur in his place and underline the limits of his influence.

That is why the chicken began to sing
High, not loud, and why transparencies
Of pipestems were his legs, his beak aloft,
His feathers lean, drawing the busy air,
And why he crossed the road.[21]

The last line evokes the well-known joke ("Why did the chicken cross the road?") that typically sets up a simple punch line. Here, though, the phrase comes at the end of a long prelude that supposedly offers the reason why the chicken took to its feet. By repurposing the joke, Miles aims to do a few things. First, she seeks to delight the reader with the pleasure of recognition, after the opportunity seemed to have passed. Second, the pedantic framing takes the joke out of the riddle by making the stock question "Why did the chicken cross the road?" a rationalization and not an opening. This, in turn, reinforces the idea that the chicken belongs to a mechanistic, predetermined system that leaves no room for pleasure, surprise, or disorder: all business all the time. Third, and most importantly, Miles exploits the joke's location to put the entrepreneur in his place and point out the limits of his influence. Though the chicken appeared to have a vast reach in the first two stanzas, the line "why he crossed the road" reminds us that his reach only extends to a single road. He may be crossing over to extend his business, but the empire remains quite narrow.

The caveat matters because Miles does not want to concede too much to the entrepreneur and his world. Her poem makes a double argument. On the one hand, Miles did believe that the business class had gained too much power, distorting and narrowing the way that citizens think of society and the relations between those in a society. Certainly, the chicken in this poem mocks the self-importance that Miles identified among entrepreneurs. At the same time, the entrepreneur is not as important as he thinks. After all, economics are only a part of life, and Miles felt it important not to grant the entrepreneurs of the world too much authority. Even as the poem regrets the degree to which the business class has infiltrated public discourse and public life, the line "why he crossed the road" reminds us that the entrepreneur's power is always less than we may feel, and definitely less than they assume.

Another poem in *Kinds of Affection* considers the flip side of this problem, by shifting from the entrepreneur's pride and influence, to the resentment that the corporate world fosters among those who remain outside its bubble of privilege. Once again, Miles resorts to absurdist contrast, by framing the language of economics within a lyric poem about Daniel Boone, the American folk hero typically described exploring and hunting on the American frontier. Behind this, there is the notion that business talk has permeated public discourse to such an extent that even folktales are no longer immune. But the primary goal is to consider how rural, lower-class Americans might feel about the increasing dominance of a cosmopolitan business class, using Daniel Boone as a representative figure.

Daniel Boone stepped up to a window
(What! a window?) with his trusty rifle,
And he shot a bear.
This was some bear.
It was a millionaire,
A Harvard, London, and a South Sea bear
A French, a football bear.

A corporate family,
And incorporate party,
Thoroughly transitized
Into his rocking chair,
Built and bureaucratized,
Daddied and deared and dared,
Indomitable bear.

What an investment
Of time, of love too,
All in one body,
A computation
Of maximal purpose,
A one-man world.

Daniel is angry
That after the eighth grade
This bear should travel
So far ahead,
Unfair
That a bear should rock so big a chair.[22]

The poem culminates with Daniel Boone's anger at the privileges that the bear, here a representative of the business class ("a millionaire, / A Harvard, London, and a South Sea bear"), has accumulated with such ease. Miles does not simply align herself with these sentiments, but she is careful to make her readers understand why Daniel would have grown so angry. The second stanza is riddled with business lingo: "corporate," "incorporate," "transitized," and "bureaucratized." These adjectives are applied to the bear and spoken with anger. Daniel resents the bear for disappearing into the world of business. The passives "transitized" and "bureaucratized" indicate that Daniel views moving up the corporate ladder as a form of submission. This idea is underlined by the slip into babyish repetition, with "Daddied and deared and dared." By the third stanza, the bear is said to have lost all agency and humanity. Time and love for him are only "investments"; a body is, amusingly, just "a computation / Of maximal purpose," whose only value lies in what it can produce. This stanza is phrased as if it offered praise ("What an investment!"), but the tone is clearly sardonic, mocking the millionaire bear using his own language.

Yet the bear is also described as "indomitable." That word suggests that the terms Daniel had applied to the bear also reflect his own powerlessness and frustration in the face of a modern, corporatized world that has left him behind. Daniel, too, has been rendered passive and robbed of agency by the modern economy. The fourth stanza drops the business lingo entirely and leaves us with a portrait of Daniel alone and "angry" at all that the bear has achieved. "Unfair / That a bear should rock so big a chair." The tone of suppressed hurt is very much Daniel's; hence why the bear's privilege is pictured through a trope of rural life, the rocking chair.

Miles resists sharing in this anger as well, perhaps because she recognized how far her own experience was, as a poet and academic living in California, from that of the rural lower class whom Daniel Boone represented. But in giving voice to these frustrations, she did acknowledge them and take them seriously. For Miles, one of the chief issues with corporatese was its exclusionary nature. Business lingo isolates a privileged class by giving its members a language to distinguish themselves from others. This discourse could only deepen social divisions and feed civil unrest—as suggested by the violence that sets the poem in motion.

Fields of Learning (1968) marks yet another turn in the way that Miles used echo and critique, particularly with regards to economic lingo. The book features a series of poems imitating academic discourses across different disciplines, from history to biology. "Economics" reads:

> A man needs access to a market of genuine price
> At which he can buy as much as he is willing to pay for.
> The right place for an item is the hands of one
> Who will pay for it at least what everyone else will.
> Price sends every item, Boeing and rutabaga, to the right place.
>
> The genuine at any one time clears the market.
> Any other price is a fraud.
> The genuine wage is a wage that clears the market.
> The correct wage equals the value of the marginal product
> As the correct price equals the marginal cost.
>
> The performance of the economy is measured along four lines,
> Use of resources, employment, goods and services,
> Equity in distribution of income, but
> Few scholars have attempted across the board
> Descriptions of conduct patterns in American markets.[23]

The poem begins with a universalizing gesture ("A man"), only to submit to a sea of economic lingo: market, price, marginal cost, resources, employment, goods, services, value, "equity in distribution of income." Throughout, the speaker remains stern and definitional about what they deem "right" and correct: "The right place for an item *is*," "The genuine wage *is*," "The correct wage *equals*." The mass of specialized vocabulary makes the poem dense and difficult to parse, yet once each sentence has been unpacked, it becomes clear that all the statements in "Economics" belong to two categories. First, there are *truisms:* statements that are so obvious they do not need to be said but that have been dressed up with technical terminology to make them appear more sophisticated. One example would be, "The right place for an item is the hands of one / Who will pay for it at least what everyone else will," which essentially says that products are made to bought by those willing to pay a fair price: an obvious and uncontroversial idea. Second, there are sentences that make dubious claims while hiding behind the veneer of a professional vocabulary. The opening lines are an example of this: "A man needs access to a market of genuine price / At which he can buy as much as he is willing to pay for." While it may be true that people do need access to a reasonable market (so that they can buy food and other essential goods), the emphasis is still odd, as though the ability to buy were a fundamental human right akin to the freedom of speech. The only human "need" that the poem acknowledges is the need to buy.

Equally dubious is the underlying principle (and assumption) that everything can be defined according to the market. The poem evokes a dark system in which all human activities and relations are understood on economic grounds. One of the more chilling manifestations of this is the analogy in the second stanza: "The correct wage equals the value of the marginal product / As the correct price equals the marginal cost." Conspicuously absent here is any mention of "the worker," who just appears obliquely via "wage" and "marginal product." In a system that thinks of value only in terms of money, the employee exists solely as a set of costs and yields (hopefully more of the latter than the former). The worker is both product and profit.

The poem ends with a move that is typical in academic writing, where the author defends her choice of topic by noting how little it has been discussed: "Few scholars have attempted across the board / Descriptions of conduct patterns in American markets." In the context of this poem, however, such distinctions feel painfully out of touch. For Miles, focusing on obscure areas in the field distracts economists and others from confronting the ethical problems with economics itself. The language, and with it the ideology, of the discipline had assumed so much authority that Miles feared it would dominate civic life. Yet as with the poem about "the entrepreneur chicken," she also put economics in its place. By devoting each poem in *Fields of Learning* to a distinct academic speech genre, she situated economics as one academic discourse among many, each of which understands the world through its own terms. "Economics" may view people as wages and profits, but the poem that follows, "History," relies on a different vocabulary. While sitting on her porch reading a history book about the Hittites, she observes a boy "trying stunts / Like bucking bronco" on his bike. For Miles, his efforts "bring to light / The practicalities of cuneiform."[24] Evidently, Miles finds the terms of this discipline less restrictive than those of economics. She derives both pleasure and insight from relating the concepts of the historical study she is reading to the sight of a boy on a bike. But the very act expresses a preference for the everyday over the specialized terms of academic discourse. It is the real-life stunts that reveal the "practicalities of the cuneiform" and not the other way around. The concepts of academese are only useful to the extent that they can be related back to practical matters and even then, only within the professional circle that employ this vocabulary. Without that connection, the terms will become, at best, dead language without any real meaning or function. At worst, they will make society even less equal, less just.

One of the hallmarks of Josephine Miles's poetry is its methodical apprehension of different types of public discourse, from bureaucratese to academese. Yet in the history of echo and critique, her most important insight—an insight that makes her a precursor to recent uses of this method—was the idea that business talk had become the dominant form of public speech in the United States and infiltrated other rhetorical genres. The language of the global corporation was now, also, the language of the president, the bureaucratic office, and the university. For Miles, the true center of power had shifted from the state to business culture, which now determined the tenor of public discourse. Clichés, she argued, were instrumental in recasting society not as a varied set of relations between citizens but as a network of buyers and sellers, over which businesses could exert control. In this regard, Miles presents a striking qualification to the narrative of the imperial presidency. To her mind, other imperial powers were at play beyond the White House, and these posed as great a threat, required as much scrutiny.

7

SEAMUS HEANEY
ON
PUBLIC TALK

The poetry of Seamus Heaney marks a significant development in the history of echo and critique, for he was the first poet to analyze extensively the infiltration of doublespeak and political clichés into ordinary language. In particular, his 1975 book *North* takes on the platitudes deployed in everyday conversations about the Irish Troubles. To him, such phrases represented the failure of a divided society at rational public discourse, trading substantive debate for evasion. But Heaney did not exempt himself from the problem. Like Randall Jarrell, Heaney recognized that he, too, risked succumbing to clichés in his writing. And like Jarrell, that awareness led him to develop near-clichés: namely, phrases that are in the neighborhood of commonplaces but that have been modified to call attention to their clichéd nature. Instead of reanimating platitudes, Heaney wished to remain vigilant about his own susceptibility to cliché when discussing public matters, and to draw his readers' attention to that risk in turn. Fittingly, Heaney also reconciles the focus of echo and critique (political clichés) with that method's chief precursor: Robert Frost, whose skeptical attitude toward conversational platitudes lay the groundwork for echo and critique. Heaney recorded the impact of political stock phrases on the discourse of everyday talk.

It may seem odd to consider an Irish poet in a book devoted mainly to authors who were either American or (like Auden) working in the United States. Yet Heaney's American connections in this period warrant his inclusion here. First, Heaney wrote the poems dealing with political clichés and everyday talk about the Troubles, eventually published in *North* (1975), while teaching as a guest lecturer at the University of California, Berkeley, from 1970 to 1971. At Berkeley, he drafted a short essay titled "Views," in which he compared the rhetoric of the Irish Republican Army to that of the Black Panthers.[1] Finally, his papers at the National Library of Ireland, Dublin, reveal that many of the poems in *North* were originally written in blank sonnets before they were revised into rhymed quatrains. In one sonnet, he refers to Robert Lowell by name and praises his use of the form in his 1973 trilogy: *History, For Lizzie and Harriet,* and *The Dolphin.*[2] From this we can conclude that Heaney's experiences in the United States, and the music of one American poet in particular, had a significant influence on his own use of echo and critique in response to the everyday talk surrounding the Irish Troubles.

Heaney's wrestling with cliché goes as far back as his first book, *Death of a Naturalist* (1966). The phrases he confronted then were not political in nature; they belonged instead to the realm of aphorism and tact. Still, his early poetry is worth discussing in brief, since it shows an awareness of his own vulnerability to platitude. In "Mid-Term Break," for example, Heaney recounts the funeral of his younger brother, killed in an accident at the age of three and a half. He draws a sharp contrast between the wordless grief of his parents and the empty condolences of his friends and neighbor. The parents can only express their grief without words, "crying" with "angry tearless sighs," because their pain cannot be put into words, and their silence is opposed to the visitors' condolences, which can only be inadequate to the situation.[3] Though the phrases Heaney quotes were clearly intended by their speakers to express sympathy for the family while tactfully avoiding a brutal description of the death itself, "sorry for your trouble" unintentionally presents the young brother's death as a minor nuisance, while "it was a hard blow" is too casual and queasily evocative of the very real blow that brought the boy to his end. Importantly, Heaney does not present this as a failure on the visitors' part. The poem is not about the attitude and speech of particular people but the general inadequacy of language when faced with a personal tragedy. The question for Heaney was how to confront his loss in a poem, which is made up only of words. At first, he tries to remain silent about his feelings and portrays the sights and sounds of the funeral without describing his reactions to them. The only exception is the word "embarrassed" in the fifth line, and even that responds to the language of the guests, not the death of his younger brother. The poem mirrors that reserve in the self-possession of its tone and the plainness of its vocabulary. The logic here goes like this: if all expressions of sadness and sympathy must falter, then perhaps a poet ought to simply report the facts of the situation and avoid feeling altogether until restraint becomes itself an expression of loss.

Heaney must have realized the limits of this, however, and the end of the poem finds him reaching for a wholly different attitude, only to be confronted with the difficulty of speaking about his loss without resorting to cliché. His account of visiting the body of his brother culminates in a single sentence, isolated into its own stanza: "A four-foot box, a foot for every year." The poet has tried so meticulously to describe these events at a remove that he falls into the tactless informality he had evoked in previous stanzas. There is but a short step from the visitor's "it was a hard blow" to the phrase "knocked him clear" which caps off the final tercet. Faced with this dead end, Heaney tries out an alternative to studied simplicity in the final line. "A four-foot box" insists on the strange and unavoidable fact of his brother's coffin through its packed sequence of alliterations, assonances, and stressed monosyllables, while the second half, "a foot for every year," eases into an iambic meter and a looser pattern of sounds. Heaney tries to make something of the coffin's factualness by reading its size as proportionate to his brother's age, and so imagining the reduction of death as a kind of growth. But there are problems with this ending. While "four-foot box" risks overinsistence on fact, "a foot for every year" skirts dangerously close to sentimentality. Both phrases could easily be criticized as clichés, not because they have been overused but because each glosses over the complexities of the poet's subject. Both adopt simplified attitude of toughness and sentimentality that Heaney hopes will give the poem a formal closure unavailable to him outside the sphere of poetry. At the same time, the fact he kept the imbalance between the two halves of the line suggests he was dissatisfied with these options as well.

Heaney's early stumbles influenced his approach to the cant surrounding the Irish Troubles. While the clichés of public talk are categorically different than those in "Mid-Term Break," his first book led him to more fully recognize poetry's own susceptibility to vague, empty language that is inadequate to the situation. Strikingly, the poem in *North* that deals most directly with political cant, "Whatever You Say Say Nothing," is one of his most widely panned, despite its thorough and subtle investigation of cliché. Richard Russell believes that Heaney does not do enough to counteract cliché or offer an alternative to it: "the poem recapitulates so many clichés that it sinks under their weight, rendered incapable of the kind of specific, memorable diction that characterizes the typical Heaney poem."[4] Dennis O'Driscoll cites the poem as an example of Heaney's ineffective attempts at public writing, arguing that it just deals with politics directly and topically, and fails to show how politics get refracted through everyday particulars: "Heaney's finest work, because it is so securely rooted in time and place, can be effortlessly and indeed unconsciously political. . . . Conversely, the poems ('Whatever You Say Say Nothing,' for instance) which are explicitly political or topical in theme are less frequently successful."[5] Yet the poem is of interest because it combines a keen attentiveness to linguistic particulars with a firm refusal to excuse himself of complicity or to believe that poetry can escape cliché entirely. The poet's insecurity, his sense of being unrooted and unable to offer a simple alternative to cliché, is integral to his political responsibility and to the strengths of this poem.

One of the main challenges that Heaney faced in taking on the clichés of everyday talk about the Irish Troubles was the fact that these expressions were designed to evade scrutiny. While some phrases may be recognizable as cliché, it is often more difficult to say what makes them clichés; and indeed, that ungraspable quality can hinder proper analysis. The following passage from the poem "Whatever You Say Say Nothing" (closing out the first section of four) captures that slipperiness.

"Oh it's disgraceful, surely, I agree."
"Where's it going to end?" "It's getting worse."
"They're murderers." "Internment, understandably."
The "voice of sanity" is getting hoarse.[6]

The phrases quoted here are recognizable as platitudes, and we are clearly meant to identify them as such. Yet it is difficult to pinpoint what makes them clichés. It cannot just be that the sentences are overused, though the word "hoarse" does suggest excess repetition as well as volume, and certainly overuse is implicit in any accusation of cliché. Heaney's point is not that the ideas contained in the phrases were valuable at some point in time and have simply been corrupted by iteration. The real issue is that this habit of speech, while easily identifiable, resists analysis or pushback. It is possible to mock the phrase "Oh it's disgraceful, surely, I agree" as platitudinous, but few would deny that the violence of the Troubles was indeed "disgraceful." These phrases get much of their power from seeming to be inarguable.

By and large, critics have tended to dismiss the quotations outright. Floyd Collins describes them as "the worn responses of Irish citizens."[7] Andrew Murphy speaks briefly of a "kind of non-committal liberal attitude."[8] Thomas C. Foster refers to "a litany of standard statements, all of them empty."[9] But this takes the informality of the phrases and assumes that it reflects the poet's attitude. Far from merely dismissing clichés, Heaney uses juxtaposition and compression to closely analyze the attitudes that are implied in them. This method allows him to examine a representative sample more closely and draw out the qualities that are manifest across several phrases.

The first effect of Heaney's compression is to emphasize the repeated use of the impersonal pronoun "it," which serves as a subject to the first three phrases: "it's disgraceful," "where's it going to end," and "it's getting worse." The repetition prompts the reader to ask what the pronoun refers to and what the speakers are lamenting so vocally. Even if we decide the citizens are all denouncing the Irish Republican Army (presumably those being "interned" are the rebels, not the police, though the speakers may also have Protestant paramilitaries in mind), "it" obscures the specific referent. Are the speakers condemning the IRA's demands, their actions, or the violence between militants and the police—the historical situation—rather than the IRA itself? To Heaney, clichés act as evasions; they enable the citizen to take up the mantle of public engagement without committing themselves to a specific position. While the speakers seem to voice strong opinions, the pronoun "it" ensures that those opinions remain safely untethered.

Evasion lies behind many of the rhetorical maneuvers in this stanza. For instance, Heaney demonstrates how certain words shroud imprecise thinking in a general impressiveness of effect. He does this by packing the longest words (with the exception of "disgraceful") into the third line and so highlighting them. The monolithic word "internment" obscures who has interned whom, and the circumstances of the internment, by sweeping all such details under a blanket nominalization. The word "understandably" generalizes the speaker's approval and frames it as a universal opinion: not "I understand internment," but "Internment, understand*ably*." By treating his beliefs as a consensus his listeners no doubt share, the speaker avoids committing personally to that position. Evasion is facilitated—indeed, clinched—by the adverbial form, which occludes the subject.

At the same time, a slight threat lingers at the back of the word "understandably." Indeed, the stanza charts the grim social dynamics implied in such phrases. Heaney takes these clichés not as conflicting sides of a debate but rather as a cluster of near-identical statements, a uniform chatter. He shows that this uniformity is motivated by a profound fear, among the citizens, that they might not actually agree with one another. Evasion becomes a way to avoid conflict. Heaney captures this in the slight hesitance underlying "Oh it's disgraceful, surely, I agree." Here "surely" means both "absolutely" and "well that *must* be so," the speaker convincing himself as the sentence unfolds.

More darkly, Heaney also shows that platitudes can reinforce a majority opinion. To say "Internment, understandably" is to imply that your listeners ought to agree, since internment is widely held to be the correct position. Heaney underlines this problem further through his precise ordering of phrases, which creates not just a uniform repetition but also a clear verbal escalation. The "it" of the first three phrases yields to a more pointed "they" in the fourth phrase, and vague laments about violence ("oh it's disgraceful") sharpen into accusations ("they're murderers") and calls for punishment ("internment"). Even if the platitudes are not part of a single conversation but rather a sample of what the poet has overheard at various times and places, the impression here is that of a crowd working itself up to violence. Heaney clearly believes that public talk can foster a mob mentality, as citizens turn against one another and exclude those who are no longer deemed acceptable members of society. The final line breaks the growing hostility by curtly pitting "hoarse" against "worse" in an off rhyme, and then turning away from the march of quotations that had threatened to overwhelm the poem, but the attempt is half-hearted and resigned.

This stanza is the centerpiece of "Whatever You Say Say Nothing," and the pivot around which the poem turns. The stanzas preceding it situate the evasions of everyday talk in the context of public discourse as a whole by echoing the stock phrases of politicians and journalists. Heaney does not claim that citizens simply repeat the clichés they hear in the news; the phrases quoted at the beginning are quite different. But he does argue that the establishment is responsible for creating a discourse that prizes evasion and shies away from transparency. To his mind, politicians and news reporters share much of the blame for modeling bad rhetorical behaviors that are then mirrored in everyday talk. This idea is introduced in the opening lines:

I'm writing just after an encounter
With an English journalist in search of "views
On the Irish thing."

Heaney begins the poem by imitating the casual style of news reports ("I'm writing just after") and then mocks a phrase used by journalists when discussing the Troubles: "views / On the Irish thing." The line break does much to take this phrase and attitude apart. "Views" opens indeterminately onto a blank space, while "the Irish thing" gets pushed and cramped into the following line. This suggests an unwillingness to address the violence head-on, as evident in the hasty reduction of the conflict to a hazily defined "thing." While many would say that the journalist's role is to report other people's views on current events and not express their own, Heaney takes that objectivity as a cop-out, an unwillingness to respond with integrity. Then, in the following stanzas, he draws a parallel to the political class whose language he believes is analogous to, and complicit with, the evasions of the media. He laments:

> the jottings and analyses
> Of politicians and newspapermen
> Who've scribbled down the long campaign from gas
> And protest to gelignite and Sten,
>
> Who proved upon their pulses "escalate,"
> "Backlash" and "crack down," "the provisional wing,"
> "Polarization" and "long-standing hate."

When he refers to "jottings and analyses," Heaney seems to have in mind the soundbites given by politicians to reporters when asked to comment on public issues, so that the two are working in tandem. The list of phrases also establishes a direct link to the clichés of small talk that he turns to later in the poem. Much like the platitudes of everyday conversation, these phrases are striking for their lack of specificity. In effect, they could be applied indiscriminately to any number of situations. Granted, the professional lingo here may seem far removed from the casual language quoted later in the poem. But Heaney argues that these two genres of public discourse share the same mechanisms and purpose. Journalists and politicians avoid controversy by relying on terms designed for most any context; likewise, citizens turn to platitudes in order to disguise their opinions. These various phrases may have a different flavor, but their purpose is one and the same: to keep them at a distance from the particulars of a given event. Indeed, Heaney is even hesitant to speak of platitudes in everyday talk as spontaneous and thus different in kind from the prepared statements of the political class:

> Yet I live here, I live here too, I sing,
>
> Expertly civil-tongued with civil neighbours
> On the high wires of first wireless reports,
> Sucking the fake taste, the stony flavours
> Of those sanctioned, old, elaborate retorts

Heaney insists on the link between the "first wireless reports" and the "old, elaborate retorts" by drawing them together with a rhyme. The two discourses are comparable in that both get deployed "expertly" and so constitute a kind of expert*ise*. The word "elaborate" may seem paradoxical when set against the clipped quality of the phrases echoed by the poet. But what Heaney seems to mean by this is "intricately designed." The clichés of everyday talk seem casual and thoughtless, but they are actually complex terms designed to protect the speaker and gain the interlocutor's assent. What's more, the impact of these phrases on society is equally severe. The word "civil," in "civil-tongued" and "civil neighbours," evokes a decline from the older sense of "civic" (having to do with public life and the citizen's responsibilities in society) to the far weaker sense of "polite" (behaving just courteously enough, and perhaps with some implicit hostility). Heaney's society is no longer bound by shared responsibilities but by the thinness of basic etiquette.

Heaney is uncertain how much sympathy to grant the citizens who make use of these clichés. He presents each person as both a victim of social pressures and an enforcer of those pressures, as exemplified by the term "sanctioned." Typically, the word denotes approval that is granted by legal or religious institutions, but the clichés of everyday talk can only be "sanctioned" by the members of a society. Citizens are subject to these practices, but they also willfully participate. It is important that Heaney does not believe the poet stands apart from these rituals, however: "Yet I live here, I live here too." He admits that he, too, is guilty of his own accusations, since he not only participates in this chatter as a private citizen but also traffics in the analogous platitudes of poetic language. The tensions just described—of sympathy, critique, and self-recrimination—come to a head in the third section with a turn to the title.

The famous

Northern reticence, the tight gag of place
And times: yes, yes. Of the "wee six" I sing
Where to be saved you only must save face
And whatever you say, you say nothing.

Heaney begins the second sentence by evoking the opening line of Virgil's *Aeneid* ("Arms and the man I sing") with the six counties of Northern Ireland ("the wee six") in place of men and arms, in order to concede his own susceptibility to cliché. He then undercuts the mock-heroics in the two lines that follow, each of which follows a split structure. The word "saved" expands to "save face," only to have its religious subtext qualified and reduced to the far paltrier sense of carefully adjusting one's language to avoid embarrassment. "Whatever you say" gets similarly whittled down to "you say nothing," with "whatever" and "nothing" pitted at opposite ends of the line. All possibilities for public expression are thereby restricted to statements that will cause little or no trouble; and what value can such statements have, the poem asks, if they are solely designed to have the slightest possible effect on their listeners?

The last sentence pivots on three possible meanings. It can be read as advice (from someone who knows the consequences of not saying the right thing to someone who does not), as a threat (say nothing, or else), or as a comment about the inevitable burdens of living in such a society (no matter what you say in Northern Ireland, you will find yourself saying nothing). The ambiguity is to the point, since advising someone to watch their tongue can function as an underhanded threat, and what is advised or threatened can congeal into an unavoidable fact of life in a given society. Heaney complicates matters further by making it unclear where he stands in relation to this final line. To a certain extent, he appears to echo a common sentiment in order to then treat it ironically. But the stanza also concludes with a powerful sense of inevitability, so that the third meaning of the phrase gets pushed to the fore. Heaney knows only too well that his lament plays into a whole culture of discontent, where public talk gets privately denounced while actions and practices remain unchanged and are, perhaps, even solidified by the belief that these problems have become inevitable. And he is equally conscious that his own words risk being just as damnable and inadequate as those of the journalist, the politician, or the citizen.

In the abstract, it may appear surprising that Heaney lamented public accord at a time when Northern Ireland suffered from such profound civil unrest. Surely even a superficial agreement is better than outright hostility. But Heaney contends that hostility does in fact subtend much of public cant and that these pressures are motivated by selfish impulses as well as political prejudice. Clichés, for him, serve less to create an appearance of social harmony and more to "save face," to protect oneself from conflict or embarrassment. Indeed, what troubles him most about the platitudes of everyday talk is the implied attitude toward and behind such phrases. "It is so disgraceful" is perhaps less objectionable as a sentence out of context than in specific contexts where it becomes both a shield and a weapon.

The next question to consider is how Heaney dismantles public cant, and its strategic use of platitude, without unwittingly resorting to cliché in his own writing as well. Edna Longley thought that Heaney failed to do this when she criticized "Whatever You Say Say Nothing" as a "clichéd condemnation of clichés."[10] To complain about platitudes can itself be a tiresome platitude. Dillon Johnston similarly argues that, "in drawing close to the violence, Heaney's sensitive ear numbs, and he mocks the evasive clichés without renewing them."[11] Granted, the charge is not entirely unfair, as there are moments where he does appear to get locked into circuitous grievances. The following lines from the poem's third section merely extend the clichés of talk with sarcastic commentary:

"Religion's never mentioned here," of course.
"You know them by their eyes," and hold your tongue.
"One side's as bad as the other," never worse.

It is clear why Heaney was reluctant, in the first section, to directly analyze phrases such as these and preferred instead to compress and juxtapose, and so work by suggestion. The second line makes explicit the warning ("hold your tongue") that was implicit in "you know them by their eyes," but as a method of analysis, paraphrase seems particularly unimaginative, since the poet tells us nothing new. "Of course," the gloss on "religion's never mentioned here" criticizes the phrase for being too much the expected thing but does nothing more with it. And "never worse" limits itself to a simple reiteration of the phrase "one side's as bad as the other." There is a tired quality to these lines that is partly intentional: Heaney wants to demonstrate how derivative the phrases are, and he emphasizes this through the repeated alteration of quote and comment, one sentence per line, in a near-perfect iambic pentameter. At the same time, Heaney's attitude borders on fatalism. If, in the first section, he had at least shown himself willing to push back against the false comforts of platitude, the lines just quoted grudgingly take these phrases to be inevitable, so that his own attitude chimes with the passivity he has elsewhere condemned.

Like Jarrell, Heaney found a way out of this dead end by creating a language that admits to the proximity of cliché and holds the risk always in view so as not to succumb to it. The complex metaphors that appear throughout *North* are the clearest examples of this approach. Heaney often takes an image that, within the sphere of poetry, has become overused to the point of simplification (in much the same way that phrases like "Oh it's disgraceful" have been overused and simplified in everyday talk), and he then proceeds to expand it, layer it with conflicting images, or complicate its function. In so doing, he does not seek to reanimate existing clichés by restoring value to them but rather to create new phrases that do not let us forget their proximity to cliché and that insist on their own compromised nature. This technique chimes with the philosophy that Heaney developed in his 1989 Oxford lectures, where he spoke of poetry as "a glimpsed alternative, a revelation of potential that is denied or constantly threatened by circumstances." That alternative, he said, depends on the separate nature of poetic language: "Poetry cannot afford to lose its fundamentally self-delighting inventiveness, its joy in being a process of language as well as a representation of things in the world."[12] Near-clichés enabled Heaney to sustain poetry's self-delighting inventiveness in the face of public cant, while at the same time insisting on his own susceptibility to platitude. Of course, one might easily accuse this of escapism as well, but near-clichés shift the relation between language and power in one important way. The platitudes Heaney condemns in "Whatever You Say Say Nothing" rob the citizens of power—over their own language and public discourse—by giving them stock sentiments they can only resort to self-consciously. Near-clichés, by contrast, restore a sense of linguistic control by modeling phrases that can be shaped, possessed, and thought over rather than submitted to by necessity.

An example of near-clichés in Heaney's writing appears in the sequence "Singing School," which deals with the Northern Irish conflict—and

Heaney's attitude toward it—from his childhood to the present day. The fourth section, "Summer 1969," focuses on his visit to Madrid as riots were breaking out in Ulster. Heaney recalls his guilt at being away from Ireland, and how that guilt deepened—and, ultimately, resolved itself—upon seeing Goya's *Shootings of the Third of May* and his so-called Pinturas Negras (Black Paintings). To him, these works offered a model of responsible artistry in time of war. He praises Goya's "nightmares, grafted to the palace wall," their depictions of "Dark cyclones," "Gigantic Chaos," and "Saturn / Jewelled in the blood of his own children."[13] As the poem comes to a close, Heaney offers the following tribute to his aesthetic approach:

> He painted with his fists and elbows, flourished
> The stained cape of his heart as history charged.

"Heart" is recognizably a cliché, with sentimental connotations of courage and passion. Heaney sets Goya's metaphorical "heart" within a broad allegorical bullfight, with Goya as the torero, his "heart" as a cape, and history as the charging bull. At first, the image may seem to state its meaning plainly (the painter resists, and escapes, the pressures of history), and indeed many critics have complained that the poem's ending oversimplifies. John Dennison, for instance, has said that "the poet or artist's endeavors are shaped by and pitched against a simple, wholly negative hypostatization of 'history.'"[14] But the individual images of cape, torero, and bull keep slipping away from the allegory in which they are encased. There is the question, first, of what the "heart" would represent as a cape in a bullfight, since the image suggests that Goya's passion allowed him to both lure and evade violence. We could make sense of this by saying Heaney admires Goya's willingness to court danger, as opposed to his own tendency to avoid conflict. But then we would have to settle the further ambiguity of his heart-cape being "stained." Stained by whose blood—the toreador's or the bull's? Has Goya been sacrificing himself to the violence of history (and if he has, how so), or has he been triumphing admirably over history? The desire to read this pair of lines as a miniature narrative is complicated by the fact that the "stain" arrives before the toreador and the bull have met, while "history" is still charging. Past and future are thereby flattened into a radically disorienting present. Here, too, we can find a way out of these paradoxes. Perhaps "stained" is simply a reference to the color of the cape, or perhaps it has been "stained" from a previous fight that keeps repeating itself. But none fit well enough for the allegory to run smoothly and transparently. "Stained" carries too strong an implication to simply refer to the color red, and thinking of the cape as "stained" from previous fights is to stretch the temporal frame of the allegory much further than can be justified for two lines.

If the allegory does cohere, it is in relation to the style of Goya's own nightmarish allegories in the Pinturas Negras, which he worked on near the end of his life, from 1819 to 1823. While the thematic implications of "Dark cyclones" and "Saturn / Jewelled in the blood of his own children" may be readily apparent, one would be hard-pressed to attribute any of these images to historical fact without feeling that one has done the works a disservice. This difficulty is borne out by Goya's critics, who have variously read the *Saturn Devouring His Own Children* painting, for example, as a reflection of the artist's physical and mental distress at the end of his life,[15] the violence of the Spanish Inquisition,[16] and the political authoritarianism of Fernando VII's regime.[17] Indeed, Heaney admires these paintings not just for the boldness and grandness of their visual style but also for their slanted approach to their historical subject matter. Goya's allegories succeed because they always elude the references they seem built to support. This idea of Goya as un-pin-down-able features prominently in the image of the cape, which the torero-artist flourishes to dodge history's charge. Heaney takes that method up in his own style at the end of the poem, with a verbal allegory that sidesteps our attempts at a plain interpretation.

Elsewhere, Heaney reworks cliché within the narrow confines of the symbol rather than the narrative expansiveness of allegory. "Exposure," the final poem in the "Singing School" sequence, also deals with the guilt that he felt for not responding publicly to the Troubles. In his Nobel Prize lecture, he read the poem in its entirety and spoke of his intentions in writing it: "What I was longing for was not quite stability but an active escape from the quicksand of relativism, a way of crediting poetry without anxiety or apology."[18] But while the poet does not express anxiety, he undoubtedly confronts the limits of his beliefs about poetry and politics, and complicates his language. Early on he mocks his desire to write apolitically and portrays himself as a caricature of the philosophic type: "I am neither internee nor informer; / An inner *émigré,* grown long-haired / And thoughtful." He goes on to describe himself as a "wood-kerne," a sixteenth-century Irish guerilla fighter for the Jacobites, "Escaped from the massacre." In the final lines, he acknowledges having missed (what he terms) "The once-in-a-lifetime portent, / The comet's pulsing rose."[19]

Surprisingly, the critics who have discussed this final line take its metaphorical properties as a given and do not question what the image points to specifically. Andrew Murphy is a good example of this tendency: "In asserting, at the close of the poem, that he has missed the 'comet's pulsing rose,' Heaney may well be ruefully acknowledging a certain sense of having failed, in *North,* adequately to trace the large-scale outlines of his country's and his community's predicament."[20] Yet for all its force and finality, the image resists literal interpretation. What did the comet portend? That he ought to speak out? But "portent" implies something that had to come to pass: an act of fate rather than a choice or an opportunity. The comet could be read as a metaphor for the Troubles, the historical event beyond the poet's control that he was expected to respond to nonetheless. But to whittle down the Troubles—a protracted civil conflict—into a single metaphorical object does not quite work, unless we are to understand there was a specific point in the Troubles where the chance to speak out became manifest, only to disappear. But why would that opportunity have passed now, in the 1970s, with the end of the conflict nowhere in sight? Moreover, to speak of the Troubles, or any point in the Troubles, as a "once-in-a-lifetime" event would have seemed dubious even to Heaney. Other events will no doubt arise over the course of his life that will demand a response from a public-minded poet.

Equally problematic is the specificity of the description. Comets are a standard trope in poetry, where they typically symbolize a sudden change in the political or social life of a nation. These symbolic properties can be traced back to Homer's *Iliad* and Athena's star-like descent from Olympus, which, as Michael Ferber points out, has long been translated into English as "comet" rather than "star."[21] William Blake's imagining of revolution as a "terror like a comet" has had particular resonances in the context of Ireland's fight for independence.[22] In short, the comet is a symbol that, through its long use, comes dangerously close to poetic cliché. Heaney

puts pressure on our expectations for this image by expanding and juxtaposing it with the image of a "pulsing rose." In so doing, he introduces a
competing symbol with romantic and erotic associations that may seem
difficult to reconcile with the political nature of the comet metaphor.
One way to make sense of the "pulsing rose" figuratively, not simply as a
reference to color, is to focus on a narrower strand of meaning: the rose as
a symbol of brevity. Heaney's once-in-a-lifetime chance passed as quickly
as the rose blooms and dies. Or we may choose to read it as an allusion to
Yeats, who often made use of rose imagery. But in Yeats as well the rose
serves an oddly transhistorical function, by giving the poet access to "an-
cient ways" of myth and allowing him to escape the pressures of contemporary politics.[23] In short, by layering a host of associations (not all of which
can be easily reconciled) into a single phrase, Heaney crafts a metaphor
that rejects any attempt to draw from it a simple or single interpretation.

There is an instructive parallel, though not an exact correspondence,
between Heaney's handling of cliché in these poems and his attitude toward the demand for public writing. Neil Corcoran has summarized the
latter thus: "'Exposure,' the culminating poem of the sequence (and of
North itself), may be regarded as the tentative, muted rejection of the
kinds of exemplary status offered by his own community and culture, and
the assertion of a new kind of exemplariness; more elusive, uncertain and
oblique, still conscious of political obligation, but aware too that the self,
if it is to be adequately realized in art, must be more than merely a socially
exemplary self."[24] "Exposure" admits to the pressure of cliché and the inevitability of cliché, and the poem also insists on pushing back. It would
be possible to speak of this in Dillon Johnston's terms as a "renewal," but
that would suggest Heaney, in dusting off clichés, wished to reestablish
their legitimacy. Instead, he complicates these images and holds them
under pressure, so that we remain conscious of their origin in cliché, their
proximity to it, and how easily they may slip back.

Heaney takes this same approach at the end of "Whatever You Say
Say Nothing," where he juxtaposes a series of near-clichés into the com-
pressed shape of a quatrain, a clear parallel to the stanza in which Heaney
reels off a sample of conversational platitudes. Interestingly, what sets this
new sequence into motion is the sight of graffiti, yet another instance of
language taken from the public sphere.

Is there a life before death? That's chalked up
In Ballymurphy. Competence with pain,
Coherent miseries, a bite and sup,
We hug our little destiny again.

One can imagine a far simpler version of those opening lines, where the graffiti is offered as a more direct, sincere, and socially conscious form of expression than the chatter of everyday conversation. But Heaney is careful not to romanticize, and his tone flattens whatever temptation the reader might have to make too much of the question, "Is there a life before death?" He had used the phrase before as the epigraph to *Wintering Out* (1972), a volume that celebrates the variety of dialects and traditions in his native province. Daniel Tobin points out that Heaney's reappropriation of the graffiti across two works "emphasizes the exploratory and provisional nature of both books as they examine and reexamine the forces of language, myth, and history as well as the responsibility of the artist."[25] It is also worth emphasizing the difference in tenor between these two instances and what it suggests about Heaney's change in focus. In *Wintering Out,* the epigraph provided a question that the poems could then attempt to answer, by asserting a culture's vitality in the face of historical challenges past and present. In *North,* the phrase takes on a more compromised and less celebratory function, as a working model for near-clichés. For Heaney, the value of this sentence lies in its counterintuitiveness. The graffitist has taken a much older question, "Is there a life after death?," and radically altered it by substituting "after" with "before" and suggesting that life in Northern Ireland is no life at all. In doing so, he echoes an expression we may have grown too comfortable with and compels us to think again, much as the poet seeks to do throughout his 1975 volume.

Heaney adopts this method in the four phrases that bring his poem to a close—all of which are in the neighborhood of cliché and seem to vaguely echo clichéd sentiments but are complicated to refocus our attention. "Competence with pain," for example, surprises by claiming that strong feeling (pain) may be compatible with workmanlike ease and familiarity (competence). One might otherwise assume that pain would be too great to allow for such ease, or that the strength of pain would demand a stronger form of mastery than mere competence. A similar trick:

"coherent miseries" awkwardly forces those disparate, plural "miseries" back into a "coherent" whole after they have been split. "A bite and sup," meanwhile, startles because of its placement in the stanza, sandwiched between "miseries" and "destiny." The arrangement puts the banality of everyday life into a bizarre contrast with the malaise going on around it. How small the routines (and comforts) of daily life seem when pitted against a background of civil strife. "We hug our little destiny again," finally, makes "destiny" small and physical, even as it mocks the sentimentality that we may wish to expend on it. Heaney creates a similar paradox between the communal pronoun "our" and the self-protective gesture of the hug: the adamant singularity of "destiny," not "destinies."

Taken as a group, these phrases express impatience with Northern Irish passivity in the face of continued violence: mere competence, small miseries and small destinies, but no action. Heaney, conscious of this risk in himself, does much to fight a linguistic form of passivity, in which talk of "pain," "misery," and "destiny" allows the poet to grow complacent. Near-clichés offer a way out of the problem he encountered throughout *North,* of simply mocking platitude without moving beyond it. Importantly, Heaney does not offer these phrases as a solution to the ills of public talk; he is too aware of the fundamental differences between poetry and conversation. He does, however, believe poetry has a distinct role to play, as a "glimpsed alternative" expanding the possibilities of public language at a time when it seems impoverished. With one important qualification. Whatever lift can be felt from "again" (the final word in "Whatever You Say Say Nothing"), whatever potential the word might have to signify renewal, must be weighed against the fact these phrases represent new clichés and not a simple avoidance of cliché, which Heaney deemed impossible. He recognizes that the language he uses to speak of current events will necessarily be as compromised as that of the politician, the news reporter, and the ordinary citizen. What he can hope to do is create a language that admits to its limitations.

Heaney's poetry is important to the history of echo and critique because it confronts head-on a consequence of the postwar thinking on public cant. If these phrases pose a particular danger because they are so easy to pick up and pass on unthinkingly, then their use cannot be contained to the political class. The rhetorical habits of evasion make their way into everyday conversations and affect the ways that ordinary citizens speak and think—or do not think—about their society. The poems of *North* are notable because they testify to the wide-reaching effects of public discourse and its corruption, extending into everyday speech. Heaney wrote these poems with no illusion that they would, as T. S. Eliot intended, "purify the dialect of the tribe." Clichés will make their way into both poetry and ordinary language regardless. But like all the other poets discussed in this book, Heaney remained hopeful that poetry might help us be more aware of political clichés and their influence on everyday talk, so that we may be always conscious of the way these phrases operate on us.

CODA

Our history of echo and critique began with World War II, the era when poets started using this method widely and made it an integral feature of contemporary writing. It will come as little surprise, then, that poets took up this method when looking back to World War II at the turn of the twenty-first century, a time when that earlier conflict was often evoked as a counterpoint to the wars in Iraq, Pakistan, and Afghanistan. To think about the Second World War meant weighing critically the terms used to defend the war then and celebrate it now. Poets instinctively gravitated toward echo and critique to perform that task, whether or not they were conscious of its origins. A recurring idea in these poems is that the popular memory of World War II has become clouded by nostalgia, spurred by the desire to find a more honorable contrast to the increasingly unpopular conflicts that America found itself mired in across the world. The apparent simplicity of the Second World War by comparison makes that nostalgia easier to carry off. With the ease of historical distance, Allied victory could supply a reassuring narrative about the triumph of good over evil. The phrase "the good war," which gained currency by the 1980s, presented the cause as irrefutably justified and the United States as undeniably in the right.[1] Many poets writing at the start of the new century chose to push back against the popular nostalgia for World War II and the patriotic clichés sustaining these fantasies, whether they had lived through the conflict (Howard Nemerov, Kenneth Koch) or were born after it (Jorie Graham). In the next several pages, I would first like to consider a few examples of this phenomenon.

Howard Nemerov, who had served as a pilot, critiqued the notion of "the good war" in a poem titled "The War in the Air," first published in the *Paris Review* in 1986 and then collected in *War Stories: Poems about Long Ago and Now* (1990). His principal argument is that Americans like to speak of World War II as a "good war" only because they were the clear victors. But that simplistic view of history required one to erase those who suffered and died in the conflict:

> That was the good war, the war we won
> As if there was no death, for goodness's sake.[2]

The first line immediately glosses "the good war" as "the war we won," to leave no doubt as to what motivates the nostalgia behind that phrase. Provocatively, "the war we won" implies a contrast with the (more numerous) campaigns that the United States did not win, suggesting that embarrassment over America's mixed military record also lies behind popular nostalgia for World War II. The next line continues the same process, revealing what the cliché obscures, but what gets brought out here is far more serious than embarrassment. Death is what a phrase like "the good war" denies, since to speak of a conflict as simply "good" necessitates forgetting those who did not make it out alive. The use of a singular abstraction ("death") rather than a plural ("As if there were no deaths") emphasizes the vastness of the loss that the United States and other Allied countries sustained even in victory. With "for goodness's sake" at the end of the line, Nemerov revisits, skeptically, the word "good" by evoking an idiom typically used to express frustration. The moral cause associated with World War II (fighting for "the good") thus gets rewritten into a phrase that rejects the notion of simple "good" in war. Rather than confront the loss and the guilt that comes with it, popular memory will prefer to dismiss those who have died from the narrative. Nemerov's poem is an argument against forgetting and an exercise in testing clichés against historical reality.

A similar goal animates Kenneth Koch's "To World War II," first published in *New Addresses* (2000). Like Nemerov, Koch aims to dispel the nostalgia surrounding the Second World War, which survives in and through clichés. Koch's critique of stock language culminates in his response to the phrase "paying my debt to society."

> If I survived
> I was "paying my debt
> To society" a paid
> Killer.[3]

The quotation marks further distance the poet and heighten the irony in his tone, leaving little doubt as to his skepticism. The gloss that follows radically revises the dynamic between soldier and society, and suggests a far darker reality. "Paying one's debt to society" presents warfare as a way for citizens to repay their society for the benefits they have received. But to Koch's mind, it is the soldiers who are being "paid"—to do the dirty work that most societies would not wish to claim for themselves, and then to keep quiet and forget. "Paid killer" draws a line connecting the soldier and the hitman, and argues that the act both are asked to perform is fundamentally the same.

Writing in the midst of the Iraq War, which sparked a reckoning about America's role in the world, Jorie Graham witnessed a resurgence of nostalgia for the Second World War. Her 2005 book *Overlord* describes Omaha Beach in Normandy and weighs its present state—a landscape adored and visited for its picturesque beauty—against its violent past. In one poem in particular, "Spoken from the Hedgerows," Graham contrasts the evasiveness of jingoistic clichés with the violence of the war itself.

> To bring back a time and place.
> A feeling. As in "we're all in this
> together." Or "the United States and her allies
>
> fought for Freedom." To bring back.
> The experience of killing and getting killed.
> Get missed. Get hit.[4]

For Graham, the idealized reminiscence of World War II is founded not on historical fact but on "a feeling," which is fallible. The clichéd phrases "we're all in this / together" and "the United States and her allies / fought for Freedom" promptly give way to harsher realities. The second instance of "To bring back," isolated as its own sentence, evokes all of the lives that, unlike "a feeling," cannot be resuscitated. "The experience of killing and getting killed" makes the violence explicit, though it does so with complex irony: "killing and getting killed" is precisely the emotion that nostalgists do *not* want to bring back. Finally, the clear parallel between "Get missed" and "Get hit," united by a single verb, reminds us that surviving the war does not mean escaping it. War has a direct and long-lasting impact even on those who come back, seemingly unscathed but haunted by "the experience of killing and getting killed" that they would much rather forget.

It is apt that poets looking back to World War II would gravitate toward a method that first entered the repertoire during the same period. This is not to say that echo and critique has become a backward-looking technique, interested only in past discourses. On the contrary, it continues to be used today by poets engaging with the political language of the present. After all, concerns about the corruption of public discourse preoccupies the intellectuals of the twenty-first century as much as it did those of the immediate postwar era. In what has often been termed a "highly polarized moment" (to quote one recent cliché), both Right and Left have been charged with using obscure jargon, weasel words, and doublespeak. Timothy Lynch, writing for the libertarian think tank the Cato Institute in 2006, criticized the doublespeak used in the "war on terror" (itself a newly minted cliché), especially the development, by the George W. Bush administration, of euphemisms to disguise interrogation practices. Of the phrase "asymmetrical warfare," he writes:

> The American prison facility at Guantanamo Bay, Cuba, has been a frequent target of criticism because of Bush administration policies concerning the detention and treatment of prisoners. Whatever one may think about those detention and treatment policies, it is clear that the U.S. military has employed doublespeak to describe events at Guantanamo. "Self-injurious behavior incidents" is the Pentagon's phrase for suicide attempts by prisoners, for example. And when three men hanged themselves in their cells, the camp commander, Rear Admiral Harry Harris, went so far as to say that the suicides were "an act of asymmetrical warfare" against the American military." Warfare? A terrorist engages in asymmetrical warfare when he straps explosives to his body and then detonates the bomb when he gets close to his human targets. But if "warfare" is stretched so far as to include an enemy's taking his own life, it is difficult to identify what actions a prisoner might engage in that would *not* constitute warfare.[5]

David Bromwich likewise critiqued President Barack Obama for continuing to use evasive language to talk about America's military actions abroad: "A thoroughgoing practice of euphemism was in fact his largest innovation in the conduct of the war. Thus the murder of bin Laden by US special forces was turned into the sentence: 'We delivered justice to bin Laden.'"[6] The harshness of Donald Trump's rhetoric might seem to set it apart from euphemism and pose a different set of problems, yet he deployed contradictory and counterfactual phrases that belonged squarely to the category of doublespeak. Indeed, George Orwell's *1984* was frequently evoked by journalists and other political commentators throughout his administration. One notorious example is the assertion by Trump's lawyer Rudy Giuliani, during an interview with Chuck Todd of *Meet the Press,* that "Truth isn't truth." *Politico* reporters Rebecca Morin and David Cohen noted: "Giuliani's observation about truth was widely mocked on Twitter. A number of those tweets focused on George Orwell's book *1984*—a novel about a totalitarian state where 'war is peace,' 'freedom is slavery' and 'ignorance is strength.' Those phrases reflect 'doublethink,' a concept whereby the enslaved citizenry is kept in check."[7]

Much like at midcentury, we find time and again the idea that the dissemination of clichés in political discourse is either a wholly new phenomenon or one that has become newly urgent. Yet we have also seen that clichés are a perennial issue for public speech: they have just assumed different forms at different times. Don Watson's argument in *Death Sentences* (2005)—that public rhetoric in the twenty-first century is marked by an uneasy alliance of political language and business talk—illustrates that tension between the persistence of cant across time and the sense of its newness.

> Political and corporate thinking have merged.... On both sides the fashion is for *strategies* and *outcomes*. The latter is a modern portmanteau to hold such words as "result," "consequence," "upshot," "product," "effect," "return," and "happenstance," which are all subtly different and don't suggest, as "outcomes" does, that everything in the world is or can be governed by *strategies*. Without *outcomes* you can't have *accountability*, another catch-all to replace more challenging concepts like integrity, honesty, decency, truth, and justice. *Accountability* makes people with the capacity to do good

fear for the consequences of doing something for which they might be held accountable. So long as it runs on the principles of *accountability,* a business or department is less likely to profess, practice, or even know anything about imagination, courage, initiative, reflection, or generosity (to name just a few), which have been priceless human qualities until now and great aids to getting at the truth. It is even possible that the fashion for *accountability* encourages the use of dead words—because what is dead contains no threat.[8]

Even as he recognizes that the dominance of clichés in public speech is not new, Watson maintains that these more recent manifestations are worse: "George Orwell was appalled by political language sixty years ago. He would be more appalled now."[9] The same will likely be said, again and again, in each passing decade.

Indeed, because political clichés continue to be a problem for civic discourse, the usefulness of echo and critique has not been lost on contemporary poets. Recent practitioners include Franny Choi, whose "On the Night of the Election" (2017) torques the slogans of the 2008 US presidential campaign against the backdrop of the 2016 election:

> everyone
> was giving up
> hope of a brand I'd
> never cared much for
> anyway, wanting to be cold-
> blooded and over all that
> hopey-changey stuff[10]

The union of politics and advertising, as evident in the campaign slogan, is crystallized by the word "brand." There is no political philosophy to be found here. *Hope* and *Change* (the slogans of Barack Obama's 2008 presidential campaign) have been reduced to empty political gestures: self-fashioning for a "brand" that has yielded much disappointment. Choi approaches these slogans not from the right but the left: specifically, as part of a younger generation that had felt inspired by the prospect of an Obama presidency and then let down by the results. For Choi, the "hope" that she and others had to "give up" was quite real, and the loss bitter in light of the slogans that had promised so much. But Choi was also writing this poem on the night of the 2016 election, when the victory of Donald Trump over Hillary Clinton spurred profound fears about the country's future. Suddenly, the desire to be cynical, almost "cold-blooded," about the Obama years felt like its own empty self-fashioning, now that the country was faced with an impending Trump regime. Choi finds herself stuck between disappointment and fear, paralyzed and unmoored.

Another recent example is Terrance Hayes's "Support the Troops!" (2010), which examines critically yet playfully the stock phrase cited in the title. Hayes responds to the imperious command in the form of a polite letter declining to lend his support and explaining the reasons why.

> I'm sorry I will not be able to support any soldiers
> at this time. I have a family and a house with slanting floors.
>
> There is a merciless dampness in the basement,
> a broken toilet, and several of the windows are painted shut.
> . . . .
>
> I realize were it not for the sacrifices of these young boys,
> America would no longer have its source
>
> of power. I have given considerable thought to your
> offer, but I simply am unable to offer my support.[11]

Ingeniously, the poem answers a specific type of cliché (the jingoistic slogan) with the stock gestures of another genre (the formal letter), by evoking its polite, conventional phrases: "I'm sorry I will not be able to support at this time," "I have given considerable thought to your offer," and "I simply am unable to offer my support." The other patriotic clichés that surface in the poem—the reference to deaths as "sacrifices," and the sentimental depiction of soldiers as "young boys"—sound even more clichéd from being set against the artificial conventions of a different discourse. At the same time, Hayes is brazenly direct, and not at all evasive, about the reason why America's military footprint is such a high priority for its government. It is the country's principal "source / of power," not really or solely part of an idealistic "fight for Freedom" abroad. By the same token, the reasons that Hayes provides for not lending his support are equally clear-eyed about the limits of his own will to protest. Hayes does not object on the basis of high-minded principles: he just has other, personal concerns to address, like "a house with slanting floors," "a broken toilet," and "several of the windows" that are "painted shut." To some extent, this shift to the domestic and the everyday is a relief from the imperious command that tries to corral each citizen into supporting an imperialistic military project. But Hayes is also making fun of his tendency, and the tendency of many other people, to bristle at jingoistic clichés before turning back to his own affairs. It is difficult to meaningfully protest a vast, systemic problem like American foreign policy, especially as an individual. Personal concerns will invariably draw us back in the end. What Hayes did feel he could do, and does here, is write a poem that renews our attention to the cliché and challenges the temptation we may feel to simply pass over it, forgetting what phrases such as these conceal and enable.

Echo and critique remains one of the most substantial ways for poets to contribute to public debate. Close attention to linguistic particulars, essential in poetry, allows writers to listen vigilantly to political discourse and identify verbal habits that have gotten so engrained as to now be invisible. Even at its most critical, though, echo and critique is always founded on a principle of dialogue. By incorporating a phrase into their writing and responding to it, poets are less apt simply to dismiss a phrase they find objectionable. This method encourages poets to weigh a phrase carefully, to think with it and through it, and not to resort to an easy verdict. For readers, echo and critique models a way of attending closely and responsibly to the clichés that saturate political discourse, without the false comfort of believing either that they can stand apart from clichés, or that we will someday be rid of them entirely. Clichés will always form a part of public speech. Because of this, echo and critique will continue to be of use for poets who wish to make sense of the discourse that surrounds us, and in which we are (often unconscious) participants.

ACKNOWLEDGMENTS

This book would not have been possible without the kindness and support of colleagues, friends, and family over the past ten years. At Boston University, where I began the research for this book, I benefited from two exceptional, and highly complementary, mentors. Bonnie Costello offered steady guidance and incisive feedback at each stage of writing and revision. Laurence Breiner was exceedingly generous with his time, expressing faith in this work and in my potential beyond it. At Boston University I had the opportunity to begin working for the Wallace Stevens Society. I would like to thank the officers—Lisa Goldfarb, Bart Eeckhout, and Glen MacLeod—for providing such a warm and supportive environment to this day. Since arriving at Austin Peay State University, I have benefited from the support of three successive department chairs: David Guest, Mercy Cannon, and Beatrix Brockman. All went above and beyond to give me the resources needed to complete this book. Finally, James Long at Louisiana State University Press has been marvelous to work with. I could not have asked for a better editor.

I am deeply grateful to my friends, whose kindness, encouragement, and sense of humor have sustained me through the past decade: Neeta Bhasin, Michael Chandler, Andrew Kostakis, Alex MacConochie, Cady Steinberg, Ben Torres, Jane Wessel, Paula White, and Jeffrey Williams. My parents, Estelle and Laurent, have been unwavering in their support, even when my goals presented numerous logistical difficulties. I would never have been able to pursue my interests without them. Finally, Chris Udal's love and patience day to day has been a refuge in more ways than I can say here.

Portions of chapter 2 first appeared as "Wistful Lies and Civil Virtues: Randall Jarrell on World War II Propaganda." *Journal of Modern Literature* 43.3 (Spring 2020): 4563.

Portions of chapter 7 first appeared as "Seamus Heaney and the Clichés of Public Talk." *Philological Quarterly* 97.1 (Winter 2018): 97–119.

————

NOTES

Introduction

1. George Orwell, *Essays* (London: Penguin, 2000), 350.

2. Orwell, *Essays,* 352.

3. Orwell, *Essays,* 348–49.

4. Orwell, *Essays,* 356.

5. Orwell, *Essays,* 356.

6. Lionel Trilling, *The Liberal Imagination* (New York: New York Review of Books, 2008), 285.

7. Hannah Arendt, *Eichmann in Jerusalem: A Report on the Banality of Evil* (New York: Viking, 1963), 43–44.

8. Herbert Marcuse, *One-Dimensional Man* (Boston: Beacon, 1964), 86.

9. Marcuse, *One-Dimensional Man,* 89.

10. Mario Pei, *Doublespeak in America* (New York: Hawthorn, 1973), 1.

11. Randall Jarrell, "Changes of Attitude and Rhetoric in Auden's Poetry," *Southern Review* 7, no. 2 (Autumn 1941): 134.

12. Jarrell, "Changes of Attitude and Rhetoric," 138.

13. Jarrell, "Changes of Attitude and Rhetoric," 139.

14. William Lutz, *Doublespeak: From "Revenue Enhancement" to "Terminal Living"* (New York: Harper and Row, 1987), 7.

15. Jonathan Swift, *The Essential Writings: Authoritative Texts, Contexts, Criticism,* ed. Claude Julien Rawson and Ian Higgins (New York: Norton, 2010), 253.

16. Thomas Paine, *Rights of Man, Common Sense, and Other Political Writings,* ed. Mark Philip (Oxford: Oxford University Press, 1995), 182.

17. George Gordon Byron, *The Complete Miscellaneous Prose,* ed. Andrew Nicholson (Oxford, UK: Clarendon, 1991), 128.

18. Gerd Horten, *Radio Goes to War: The Cultural Politics of Propaganda during World War II* (Berkeley: University of California Press, 2002), 13–14.

19. Mitchell Charnley, *News by Radio* (New York: Macmillan, 1948), 8–9.

20. Michael Warner, "Publics and Counterpublics," *Public Culture* 14, no. 1 (2002): 81 and 58.

21. Warner, "Publics and Counterpublics," 86.

22. Rita Felski, *The Limits of Critique* (Chicago: University of Chicago Press, 2015), 12.

23. The phrase—T. S. Eliot's translation of Stéphane Mallarmé—is spoken famously by the "compound ghost" in "Little Gidding" (see Eliot, *Collected Poems and Plays* [London: Faber and Faber, 1969], 194). For a broader view of the historical impulses behind the modernist will to "purify" language, see Morag Shiach, "'To Purify the Dialect of the Tribe': Modernism and Language Reform," *Modernism/modernity* 14, no. 1 (January 2007): 21–34.

24. See William Wordsworth's preface to *Lyrical Ballads, with Pastoral and Other Poems* (1802), in which he defends "fitting to metrical arrangement a selection of the real language of men in a state of vivid sensation" (Wordsworth, *The Major Works*, ed. Stephen Gill [Oxford: Oxford University Press, 1984], 595).

25. Excerpts are taken from Robert Frost, *The Poetry of Robert Frost*, ed. Edward Connery Lathem (New York: Henry Holt, 1979), 33–34.

26. Gwendolyn Brooks, *In Montgomery* (Chicago: Third World, 2003), 1.

27. Kenneth Goldsmith, *Uncreative Writing* (New York: Columbia University Press, 2011), 1.

28. Kenneth Goldsmith, *Seven American Deaths and Disasters* (New York: powerHouse, 2013), 127.

29. Donald Davie, *Purity of Diction in English Verse* (London: Routledge, 1967), 31.

30. Christopher Ricks, *The Force of Poetry* (Oxford, UK: Clarendon, 1984), 356 and 359.

31. Jonathan Culler, "Poésie et cliché chez Baudelaire," in *Le Cliché*, ed. Gilles Mathis (Toulouse: Presses Universitaires du Mirail, 1998), 211.

32. Edna Longley, *Poetry in the Wars* (Newark: University of Delaware Press, 1987), 229.

33. John Shoptaw, *On the Outside Looking Out* (Cambridge, MA: Harvard University Press, 1994), 133.

34. Willard Spiegelman, *The Didactic Muse: Scenes of Instruction in Contemporary American Poetry* (Princeton, NJ: Princeton University Press, 1989), 6.

1. W. H. Auden on Bureaucratese

1. See Aidan Wasley's study of Auden's American influence in *The Age of Auden: Postwar Poetry and the American Scene* (Princeton, NJ: Princeton University Press, 2011).

2. Jarrell, "Changes of Attitude and Rhetoric," 340 and 341.

3. Jarrell, "Changes of Attitude and Rhetoric," 341.

4. R. Clifton Spargo, *The Ethics of Mourning: Grief and Responsibility in Elegiac Literature* (Baltimore, MD: Johns Hopkins University Press, 2004), 209–10.

5. Patrick Deer, "Auden and Wars," in *W. H. Auden in Context*, ed. Tony Sharpe (Cambridge: Cambridge University Press, 2013), 150.

6. Humphrey Carpenter, *W. H. Auden: A Biography* (London: Unwin, 1981), 206–22.

7. W. H. Auden, *Selected Poems,* ed. Edward Mendelson (New York: Vintage, 2007), 57.

8. George Orwell, "Political Reflections on the Crisis," *Adelphi,* December 1938, 110.

9. Orwell, *Essays,* 122–23.

10. Orwell, *Essays,* 359.

11. Orwell, *Essays,* 357.

12. Auden to Monroe K. Spears, quoted in Anthony Hecht, *The Hidden Law: The Poetry of W. H. Auden* (Cambridge, MA: Harvard University Press, 1993), 130–31.

13. Auden, *Selected Poems,* 57.

14. Auden, *Selected Poems,* 57.

15. W. H. Auden, *The Complete Works of W. H. Auden,* vol. 3, ed. Edward Mendelson (Princeton, NJ: Princeton University Press, 2008), 332.

16. W. H. Auden, foreword to *Collected Shorter Poems* (London: Faber and Faber, 1966), 15.

17. Bonnie Costello, *The Plural of Us: Poetry and Community in Auden and Others* (Princeton, NJ: Princeton University Press, 2007), 168.

18. Auden, *Selected Poems,* 93.

19. Sinclair Lewis's novel *It Can't Happen Here,* which imagines the election of a totalitarian demagogue to the US presidency, appeared in 1935.

20. Auden, *Complete Works,* 2:178.

21. Søren Kierkegaard, *The Living Thoughts of Kierkegaard* (New York: David McKay, 1952), 43.

22. Jahan Ramazani, *Poetry of Mourning: The Modern Elegy from Hardy to Heaney* (Chicago: University of Chicago Press, 1994), 180.

23. Auden, *Selected Poems,* 93.

24. Auden, *Selected Poems,* 93.

25. Auden, *Selected Poems,* 95 and 97.

26. Auden, *Selected Poems,* 96.

27. Some examples from journalists, philosophers, sociologists, and psychoanalysts: "Many of his behavior reactions are directed toward and upon the social environment which environment receives and mediates many of the influences exerted by nature. Let us note some of the ways nature influences collective man" (John Morris Gillette and James Melvin Reinhardt, *Current Social Problems* [New York: American Book Company, 1933], 41); "The aim of Bolshevism is of a diametrically opposite character: a collectivized man, a collective man" (Arthur Feiler, *The Experiment of Bolshevism* [London: G. Allen and Unwin, 1939], 227); "We must come to see that there are more ideals for collective man as well as for the individual" (John Herman Randall, *A World Community: The Supreme Task of the Twentieth Century* [New York: Frederick A. Stokes, 1930], 85); "But if, on the other hand, people crowd together and form a mob, then the dynamics of the collective man are set free—beasts or demons which lie dormant in every person till he

is part of a mob" (Carl Jung, *Psychology and Religion* [New Haven, CT: Yale University Press, 1938], 15).

28. Antonio Gramsci, *Selections from Prison Notebooks,* ed. and trans. Quintin Hoare and Geoffrey Nowell Smith (New York: International, 1971), 348.

29. William Henry Chamberlin, *The Confessions of an Individualist* (New York: Macmillan, 1940), 288.

30. Hecht, *The Hidden Law,* 160.

31. Auden, *Selected Poems,* 96.

32. Stephanie Burt, "'September 1, 1939' Revisited: Or, Poetry, Politics, and the Idea of the Public," *American Literary History* 15, no. 3 (2003): 536.

33. Jarrell, "Changes of Attitude and Rhetoric," 139.

34. Michael Murphy, "Neoclassicism, Late Modernism, and W. H. Auden's 'New Year Letter,'" *Cambridge Quarterly* 33, no. 2 (2004): 110.

35. Edward Mendelson, *Early Auden, Later Auden: A Critical Biography* (Princeton, NJ: Princeton University Press, 2017), 428.

36. Auden, *Collected Poems,* 199.

37. Peter Edgerly Finchow, *W. H. Auden: Contexts for Poetry* (Newark: University of Delaware Press, 2002), 177.

38. Carpenter, *Auden: A Biography,* 287.

39. Auden, *Selected Poems,* 206 and 207.

40. Auden, *Selected Poems,* 89.

41. Auden, *Complete Works,* 2:7.

2. Randall Jarrell on War Propaganda and the American Soldier

1. See Melissa Dinsman, *Modernism at the Microphone: Radio, Propaganda, and Literary Aesthetics during World War II* (London: Bloomsbury, 2015); Matthew Feldman, *Ezra Pound's Fascist Propaganda, 1935–45* (Basingstoke, UK: Palgrave, 2013); and Susan Schweik, *A Gulf So Deeply Cut: American Women Poets and the Second World War* (Madison: University of Wisconsin Press, 1991).

2. Horten, *Radio Goes to War,* 41.

3. Allan M. Winkler, *The Politics of Propaganda: The Office of War Information, 1942–1945* (New Haven, CT: Yale University Press, 1978), 1.

4. Eduard C. Lindeman and Clyde R. Miller, introduction to *War Propaganda and the United States,* ed. Harold Lavine and James Wechsler (New Haven, CT: Yale University Press, 1940), ix.

5. Marianne Moore, *New Collected Poems,* ed. Heather Cass White (New York: Farrar, Straus and Giroux, 2017), 387. For a history of the poem, its composition, and its variants, see Fiona Green, "Locating the Lyric: Marianne Moore, Elizabeth Bishop

and the Second World War," in *Locations of Literary Modernism: Region and Nation in British and American Modernist Poetry,* ed. Alex Davis and Lee M. Jenkins (Cambridge: Cambridge University Press, 2000), 211–12; and Robin Schulze, "How Not to Edit: The Case of Marianne Moore," *Textual Cultures: Texts, Contexts, Interpretation* 2, no. 1 (spring 2007): 129–30.

6. Judith Summer, *Plants Go to War: A Botanical History of World War II* (Jefferson, NC: McFarland, 2019), 32–50.

7. Ogden Nash, "My Victory Garden," *Home & Garden,* November 1943, 63.

8. Randall Jarrell, *Randall Jarrell's Letters: An Autobiographical and Literary Selection,* ed. Mary Jarrell (Wilmington, MA: Houghton Mifflin, 1985), 103–4.

9. Lorrie Goldensohn, *Dismantling Glory: Twentieth-Century Soldier Poetry* (New York: Columbia University Press, 2013), 200.

10. Randall Jarrell, *The Complete Poems* (New York: Farrar, Straus and Giroux, 1981), 189.

11. William H. Pritchard, *Randall Jarrell: A Literary Life* (New York: Farrar, Straus and Giroux, 1990), 99.

12. Jarrell, *Complete Poems,* 143.

13. Diederik Oostdijk, *Among the Nightmare Fighters: American Poets of World War II* (Columbia: University of South Carolina Press, 2011), 8.

14. W. S. Graham, "It All Comes Back to Me Now," *Poetry* 72, no. 6 (September 1948): 305.

15. James Dickey, "Randall Jarrell," in *Randall Jarrell, 1914–1965,* ed. Robert Lowell, Peter Taylor, and Robert Penn Warren (New York: Farrar, Straus and Giroux, 1967), 44.

16. Paul Fussell, *Wartime: Understanding and Behavior in the Second World War* (Oxford: Oxford University Press, 1989), 67.

17. Suzanne Ferguson, *The Poetry of Randall Jarrell* (Baton Rouge: Louisiana State University Press, 1971), 84.

18. Jarrell, *Kipling, Auden & Co.* (New York: Farrar, Straus and Giroux, 1980), 129.

19. Jarrell, *Complete Poems,* 169.

20. Jarrell, *Complete Poems,* 197.

21. *A Challenge to Democracy* (The War Relocation Authority, 1944).

22. Helen Vendler, *Part of Nature, Part of Us: Modern American Poets* (Cambridge, MA: Harvard University Press, 1980), 112.

23. Richard Fein, "Randall Jarrell's World of War," in *Critical Essays on Randall Jarrell,* ed. Suzanne Ferguson (Boston: G. K. Hall, 1983), 148–49.

24. *Women in Defense,* dir. John Ford (Office for Emergency Management, 1941).

25. Jarrell, *Complete Poems,* 149.

26. Benjamin Friedlander, "The Best Years of Our Lives: Randall Jarrell's War Poetry," in *Reading the Middle Generation Anew: Culture, Community and Form in Twentieth-Century Poetry,* ed. Eric Haralson (Iowa City: University of Iowa Press, 2006), 102.

27. Jarrell, *Complete Poems,* 145–46.

28. *New York Times,* January 18, 1943.

29. *New York Times,* March 18, 1943.

30. *New York Times,* November 3, 1944.

31. Stephanie Burt, *Randall Jarrell and His Age* (New York: Columbia University Press, 2002), 223–23.

32. Jarrell, *Complete Poems,* 147.

33. Jarrell, *Complete Poems,* 170.

34. Jarrell, *Complete Poems,* 150.

35. Jarrell, *Complete Poems,* 153.

36. Jarrell, *Complete Poems,* 204.

3. Langston Hughes on War Propaganda and Racial Injustice

1. Joseph McLaren, *Langston Hughes, Folk Dramatist in the Protest Tradition, 1921–1943* (Westport, CT: Greenwood, 1997), 39.

2. For a detailed account of McCarthy's response to Hughes's poetry, see chapter 5, "Back in the USSA: Joe McCarthy's Mistranslations," in Vera M. Kutzinski, *The Worlds of Langston Hughes: Modernism and Translation in the Americas* (Ithaca, NY: Cornell University Press, 2012), 184–220.

3. W. E. B. Du Bois, "Criteria of Negro Art," in *The New Negro: Readings on Race, Representation, and African American Culture, 1892–1938,* ed. Henry Louis Gates Jr. and Gene Andrew Jarrett (Princeton, NJ: Princeton University Press, 2007), 259.

4. See quotes by George E. Gordon Catlin, Eduard C. Lindeman, and Clyde R. Miller in chapter 2 of this work.

5. Langston Hughes, "Art and Integrity," *Chicago Defender,* October 20, 1945, 121.

6. Rochelle Gibson, "This Week's Personality," *Saturday Review,* April 19, 1951, 63.

7. Langston Hughes, *I Wonder as I Wander: An Autobiographical Journey* (New York: Farrar, Straus and Giroux, 2015), 173.

8. Langston Hughes, *The Collected Poems of Langston Hughes,* ed. Arnold Rampersad (New York: Vintage, 1994), 574.

9. Arnold Rampersad, *1914–1967: I Dream a World,* vol. 2 of *The Life of Langston Hughes* (Oxford: Oxford University Press, 2002), 39.

10. McLaren, *Langston Hughes, Folk Dramatist,* 156.

11. Rampersad, *Life of Langston Hughes,* 35.

12. Franklin D. Roosevelt, "State of the Union Message to Congress ('The Four Freedoms'), Washington, D.C., January 6, 1941," in *Franklin Delano Roosevelt: Great Speeches,* ed. John Grafton (New York: Dover, 1999), 92–100. For an example of a poster, see *Four Freedoms* (Washington, DC: Office of War Information, 1943).

13. Langston Hughes, *Gospel Plays, Operas, and Later Dramatic Works,* ed. Leslie Catherine Sanders, vol. 6 of *The Collected Works of Langston Hughes* (Columbia: University of Missouri Press, 2004), 461–62.

14. McLaren, *Langston Hughes, Folk Dramatist,* 156.

15. Hughes, *Collected Poems,* 221.

16. Hughes, *Collected Poems,* 569.

17. See Frederick Douglass, "The Color Line," *North American Review* 132 (1881): 567–77. W. E. B. Du Bois makes use of the phrase repeatedly in *The Souls of Black Folk* (1903).

18. Hughes, *Collected Poems,* 238.

19. Hughes, *Collected Poems,* 288–89.

20. Hughes, *Collected Poems,* 291.

21. Hughes, *Collected Poems,* 289.

22. Hughes, *Collected Poems,* 562.

4. Claude McKay on the Political Clichés of the Home Front

1. Claude McKay to Francine Budgen, August 1920, quoted in Wayne F. Cooper, *Claude McKay, Rebel Sojourner in the Harlem Renaissance: A Biography* (Baton Rouge: Louisiana State University Press, 1996), 130.

2. McKay, "Soviet Russia and the Negro," *Crisis,* December 1923, 61.

3. McKay, "Soviet Russia and the Negro," *Crisis,* December 1923, 61.

4. McKay, "Soviet Russia and the Negro," *Crisis,* December 1923, 61.

5. Claude McKay, *Complete Poems,* ed. William J. Maxwell (Champaign: University of Illinois Press, 2004), 177–78.

6. Cooper, *Claude McKay, Rebel Sojourner,* 100.

7. Tyrone Tillery, *Claude McKay: A Black Poet's Struggle for Identity* (Amherst: University of Massachusetts Press, 1992), 35.

8. Jean Wagner, *Black Poets of the United States: From Paul Laurence Dunbar to Langston Hughes* (Champaign: University of Illinois Press, 1973), 230.

9. Tillery, *Claude McKay,* 37.

10. W. E. B. Du Bois, review of *Home to Harlem,* by Claude McKay, *Crisis* 35 (1928): 202.

11. McKay to Du Bois, quoted in *The Passion of Claude McKay: Selected Poetry and Prose, 1912–1948,* ed. Wayne F. Cooper (New York: Schocken, 1973), 150.

12. Claude McKay, "The Negro Writer to His Critics," in *The New Negro: Readings on Race, Representation, and African American Culture, 1892–1938,* ed. Henry Louis Gates Jr. and Gene Andrew Jarrell (Princeton, NJ: Princeton University Press, 2007), 390.

13. McKay, "The Negro Writer to His Critics," 390.

14. McKay, "The Negro Writer to His Critics," 391.

15. McKay, *A Long Way from Home,* ed. Gene Andrew Jarrett (New Brunswick, NJ: Rutgers University Press, 2007), 28.

16. McKay, *A Long Way from Home,* 140.

17. McKay, *A Long Way from Home,* 187.

18. McKay, "Soviet Russia and the Negro," 61.

19. McKay, *Complete Poems,* 251.

20. "In the eighty years preceding Franklin Delano Roosevelt's election in 1932, the phrase appeared some 725 times in the pages of the *New York Times,* generally in either the negative ('not the American way') or the plural ('American ways and customs'). In the ten years following, it made some 2,230 appearances in the newspaper's pages and was frequently capitalized. Books began to appear entitled simply *The American Way* or *The American Way of Life.* Before 1933, only two volumes had used the phrase in their titles" (Wendy L. Wall, *Inventing the "American Way": The Politics of Consensus from the New Deal to the Civil Rights Movement* [Oxford: Oxford University Press, 2009], 15).

21. David Cort, "Democracy, Unlimited: Hitler Talks of His 'New Revolution' but America Says It's Tyranny and to Hell with It," *Life,* August 19, 1940, 70.

22. "Curran Demands End of 'Red Threat': Urges Republican Victory as Only Way to Put Down Communism in U.S.," *New York Times,* November 5, 1944, 43.

23. McKay, *Complete Poems,* 244.

24. McKay, *Complete Poems,* 244–45.

25. McKay, *Complete Poems,* 253.

26. McKay, *Complete Poems,* 260.

27. McKay, *Complete Poems,* 252.

28. McKay, *Complete Poems,* 267.

29. McKay, *Complete Poems,* 256.

30. Barbara J. Griffin, "Claude McKay: The Evolution of a Conservative," *CLA Journal* 36, no. 2 (December 1992): 162–63.

5. Robert Lowell on Political Speeches

1. Robert Lowell, *Collected Poems,* ed. Frank Bidart and David Gewanter (New York: Farrar, Straus and Giroux, 2007), 385.

2. Lowell, *Collected Poems,* 376.

3. William James, *Essays in Religion and Morality,* vol. 9 of *The Works of William James,* ed. Frederick Burkhardt and John Joseph McDermott (Cambridge, MA: Harvard University Press, 1982), 65.

4. Robert Lowell, *Collected Prose,* ed. Robert Giroux (New York: Farrar, Straus and Giroux, 1990), 165.

5. Lowell, *Collected Prose,* 165,

6. Ian Hamilton, *Robert Lowell: A Biography* (New York: Random House, 1982), 68, 366–67, 375, and 382.

7. Lowell, *Collected Poems,* 384, 803, and 838.

8. For a full account of the protests, see Stefan M. Bradley, *Harlem vs. Columbia University* (Urbana: University of Illinois Press, 2009).

9. Lowell, *Collected Poems,* 1113.

10. H. W. Brands, *The Wages of Globalism: Lyndon Johnson and the Limits of American Power* (Oxford: Oxford University Press, 1995), 76.

11. Lyndon B. Johnson, "Commencement Address at Catholic University, June 6, 1965," in *Public Papers of the Presidents of the United States: Lyndon B. Johnson, 1965* (Washington, DC: Federal Register Division, National Archives and Records Service, General Services Administration, 1966), 643.

12. 1 Isaiah 16–18 (KJV).

13. William Safire, *Safire's Political Dictionary* (New York: Oxford University Press, 2008), 136.

14. Johnson, quoted in Robert Dallek, *Lone Star Rising,* vol. 1 of *Lyndon Johnson and His Times, 1908–1960* (New York: Oxford University Press, 1991), 463.

15. 1 Isaiah 18–20 (KJV).

16. "Text of Truman's Speech Telling of U.S. Fight on Communists," *New York Times,* April 25, 1940.

17. "Text of Eisenhower's Speech on the Mutual Security Program," *New York Times,* May 3, 1960; "Text of Kennedy's Address to the Nation on His Talks in Europe," *New York Times,* June 7, 1961.

18. "Text of Johnson's Address to A.P. on Nuclear Cuts and U.S. Foreign Policy," *New York Times,* April 21, 1964.

19. "Excerpts from Johnson Vietnam Speech," *New York Times,* May 18, 1966.

20. "Address by President Johnson on China," *New York Times,* July 13, 1966.

21. Lowell, *Collected Poems,* 387.

22. John Crick, *Robert Lowell* (Edinburgh: Oliver and Boyd, 1974), 107.

23. "Text of Wicks' Keynote Address to G.O.P.," *New York Times,* September 7, 1950.

24. Lowell, *Collected Prose,* 270.

25. Samuel Eliot Morrison, *The Oxford History of the American People* (New York: Oxford University Press, 1965), 42, 57, 68–69, and 111.

26. Jeremy Black, *War for America: The Fight for Independence 1775–1783* (New York: St. Martin's, 1991), 177–78.

27. Lowell, *Collected Poems,* 385.

28. Walter Lippmann, "The All-Purpose Myth," *Newsweek,* May 24, 1965, 23.

29. "Harrison Says Go On: He Speaks at the Paris Banquet on Expansion," *Washington Post,* July 5, 1899.

30. Johnson, quoted in Michael A. Weatherson and Hal W. Bochin, *Hiram Johnson: Political Revivalist* (Boston: United Press of America, 1995), 90.

31. "Text of Herbert Hoover's Address on 'the Question of Peace,'" *New York Times,* March 29, 1941.

32. Paul Potter, quoted in Michael W. Flamm and David Steigerwald, *Debating the 1960s: Liberal, Conservative, and Radical Perspectives* (Lanham, MD: Rowman and Littlefield, 2008), 95.

33. David Farber, *The Age of Great Dreams: America in the 1960s* (New York: Hill and Wang, 1994), 138.

34. William Doreski, *The Years of Our Friendship: Robert Lowell and Allen Tate* (Jackson: University Press of Mississippi, 1990), 172–73.

35. Hamilton, *A Biography,* 329.

6. Josephine Miles on Business Talk

1. Jessica Nelson North, "Josephine Miles," in *Trial Balances,* ed. Ann Winslow (New York: Macmillan, 1935), 24.

2. Helen Vendler, "A Quarter of Poetry," review of *To All Appearances: Poems New and Selected* by Josephine Miles, *New York Times,* April 6, 1975.

3. Josephine Miles, *The Continuity of Poetic Language* (New York: Octagon, 1965), 1.

4. Zofia Burr, *Of Women, Poetry, and Power: Strategies of Address in Dickinson, Miles, Brooks, Lorde, and Angelou* (Urbana: University of Illinois Press, 2002), 69.

5. Erik Muller, *Josephine Miles* (Boise, ID: Boise State University Press, 2005), 11.

6. Naomi Clark, "Interview with Josephine Miles," in *The West,* vol. 1 of *Woman Poet* (Reno, NV: Regional Editions), 22.

7. Josephine Miles, *Collected Poems: 1930–83* (Urbana: University of Illinois Press, 1983), 137.

8. Trilling, *The Liberal Imagination,* 285.

9. Marcuse, *One-Dimensional Man,* 103

10. Pei, *Doublespeak in America,* 4.

11. Hugh Rawson, *A Dictionary of Euphemisms & Other Doubletalk* (New York: Crown, 1981), 3–4.

12. John A. Barry, *Technobabble* (Cambridge, MA: Massachusetts Institute of Technology Press, 1993), 5.

13. Don Watson, *Death Sentences: How Clichés, Weasel Words, and Management-Speak Are Strangling Public Language* (New York: Gotham, 2005), 43–44.

14. Lisa M. Steinman, "Putting on Knowledge with Power: The Poetry of Josephine Miles," *Chicago Review* 37, no. 1 (winter 1990): 135.

15. Josephine Miles, *Civil Poems* (Berkeley, CA: Oyez, 1966), 8.

16. Franklin D. Roosevelt, quoted in Peter Gardella, *American Civil Religion: What Americans Hold Sacred* (New York: Oxford University Press, 2013), 257.

17. Miles, *Civil Poems,* 9.

18. Josephine Miles, *Kinds of Affection* (Middletown, CT: Wesleyan University Press, 1967), 11.

19. Miles, *Kinds of Affection,* 33.

20. Muller, *Josephine Miles,* 41.

21. Miles, *Kinds of Affection,* 33.

22. Miles, *Kinds of Affection,* 47.

23. Josephine Miles, *Fields of Learning* (Berkeley, CA: Oyez, 1968), 10.

24. Miles, *Fields of Learning,* 11.

7. Seamus Heaney on Public Talk

1. Seamus Heaney Literary Papers, National Library of Ireland, Dublin, MS 49, 493 / 141.

2. Heaney Literary Papers, MS 49, 493 / 37.

3. All excerpts are taken from Seamus Heaney, *Death of a Naturalist* (London: Faber and Faber, 1966), 15.

4. Richard Rankin Russell, *Poetry and Peace: Michael Longley, Seamus Heaney, and Northern Ireland* (Notre Dame, IN: University of Notre Dame Press, 2010), 234.

5. Dennis O'Driscoll, "Heaney in Public," in *The Cambridge Companion to Seamus Heaney,* ed. Bernard O'Donoghue (Cambridge: Cambridge University Press, 2009), 67.

6. All excerpts are taken from Heaney, *North* (London: Faber and Faber, 1975), 52–55.

7. Floyd Collins, *Seamus Heaney: The Crisis of Identity* (Newark: University of Delaware Press, 2003), 100.

8. Andrew Murphy, *Seamus Heaney* (London: Northcote House, 2000), 45.

9. Thomas C. Foster, *Seamus Heaney* (Boston: Twayne, 1989), 72.

10. Longley, "Fire and Air," *Honest Ulsterman* 50 (winter 1975): 182.

11. Dillon Johnston, *Irish Poetry after Joyce* (Syracuse, NY: Syracuse University Press, 1997), 146.

12. Seamus Heaney, *The Redress of Poetry* (New York: Farrar, Straus and Giroux, 1996), 4 and 5.

13. Heaney, *North,* 64–65.

14. Dennison, *Heaney and the Adequacy of Poetry,* 17.

15. Folke Nordström, *Goya, Saturn, and Melancholy: Studies in the Art of Goya* (Stockholm: Almqvist and Wiksell, 1962), 220–21.

16. Albert Boime, *Art in an Age of Counterrevolution 1815–1848* (Chicago: University of Chicago Press, 2004), 112–13.

17. Michelle Facos, *An Introduction to Nineteenth-Century Art* (New York: Routledge, 2011), 93.

18. Heaney, *Crediting Poetry: The Nobel Lecture* (New York: Farrar, Straus and Giroux, 2014), 14.

19. Heaney, *North,* 68.

20. Murphy, *Seamus Heaney,* 53.

21. William Blake, *Complete Poetry and Prose* (Berkeley: University of California Press, 1982), 53.

22. Michael Ferber, *Dictionary of Literary Symbols* (Cambridge: Cambridge University Press, 2007), 156.

23. See, by way of example, "To the Rose upon the Rood of Time," in *Yeats' Poems,* ed. A. Norman Jeffares (Houndmills, UK: Macmillan, 1996), 65.

24. Neil Corcoran, "Seamus Heaney and the Art of the Exemplary," *Yearbook of English Studies* 17 (1987): 124.

25. Daniel Tobin, *Passage to the Center: Imagination and the Sacred in the Poetry of Seamus Heaney* (Lexington: University Press of Kentucky, 1999), 76.

Coda

1. See Studs Terkel, *The Good War: An Oral History of World War II* (New York: Pantheon, 1984).

2. Howard Nemerov, *War Stories: Poems about Long Ago and Now* (Chicago: University of Chicago Press, 1990), 31.

3. Kenneth Koch, *New Addresses* (New York: Knopf, 2000), 13.

4. Jorie Graham, *Overlord* (New York: HarperCollins, 2005), 40.

5. Timothy Lynch, "Doublespeak and the War on Terrorism," *Cato Institute Briefing Papers* 98 (September 6, 2006): 4.

6. David Bromwich, *American Breakdown: The Trump Years and How They Befell Us* (New York: Verso, 2019), xx–xxi.

7. Rebecca Morin and David Cohen, "Giuliani: 'Truth Isn't Truth,'" *Politico* (August 19, 2018), https://www.politico.com/story/2018/08/19/giuliani-truth-todd-trump-788161.

8. Watson, *Death Sentences,* 106.

9. Watson, *Death Sentences,* 118.

10. Franny Choi, "On the Night of the Election," BuzzFeed, April 20, 2017, https://www.buzzfeednews.com/article/poetfrannychoi/poem-on-the-night-of-the-election-by-franny-choi.

11. Terrance Hayes, *Lighthead* (New York: Penguin, 2010), 75–76.

BIBLIOGRAPHY

"Address by President Johnson on China." *New York Times,* July 13, 1966.

Arendt, Hannah. *Eichmann in Jerusalem: A Report on the Banality of Evil.* New York: Viking, 1963.

Auden, W. H. *Collected Shorter Poems.* London: Faber and Faber, 1966.

———. *The Complete Works of W. H. Auden.* Edited by Edward Mendelson. 6 vols. Princeton, NJ: Princeton University Press, 1997–2015.

———. *Selected Poems.* Edited by Edward Mendelson. New York: Vintage, 2007.

Barry, John A. *Technobabble.* Cambridge, MA: Massachusetts Institute of Technology Press, 1993.

Black, Jeremy. *War for America: The Fight for Independence 1775–1783.* New York: St. Martin's, 1991.

Blake, William. *Complete Poetry and Prose.* Berkeley: University of California Press, 1982.

Boime, Albert. *Art in an Age of Counterrevolution 1815–1848.* Chicago: University of Chicago Press, 2004.

Bradley, Stefan M. *Harlem vs. Columbia University.* Urbana: University of Illinois Press, 2009.

Brands, H. W. *The Wages of Globalism: Lyndon Johnson and the Limits of American Power.* Oxford: Oxford University Press, 1995.

Bromwich, David. *American Breakdown: The Trump Years and How They Befell Us.* New York: Verso, 2019.

Brooks, Gwendolyn. *In Montgomery.* Chicago: Third World, 2003.

Burr, Zofia. *Of Women, Poetry, and Power: Strategies of Address in Dickinson, Miles, Brooks, Lorde, and Angelou.* Urbana: University of Illinois Press, 2002.

Burt, Stephanie. *Randall Jarrell and His Age.* New York: Columbia University Press, 2002.

———. "'September 1, 1939' Revisited: Or, Poetry, Politics, and the Idea of the Public." *American Literary History* 15, no. 3 (2003): 533–59.

Byron, George Gordon. *The Complete Miscellaneous Prose.* Edited by Andrew Nicholson. Oxford, UK: Clarendon, 1991.

Carpenter, Humphrey. *W. H. Auden: A Biography.* London: Unwin, 1981.

A Challenge to Democracy. The War Relocation Authority, 1944.

Chamberlin, William Henry. *The Confessions of an Individualist.* New York: Macmillan, 1940.

Charnley, Mitchell. *News by Radio.* New York: Macmillan, 1948.

Choi, Franny. "On the Night of the Election." BuzzFeed, April 20, 2017. https://www.buzzfeednews.comarticle/poetfrannychoi/poem-on-the-night-of-the-election-by-franny-choi.

Clark, Naomi. "Interview with Josephine Miles." In *The West,* vol. 1 of *Woman Poet.* Reno, NV: Regional Editions, 1980.

Collins, Floyd. *Seamus Heaney: The Crisis of Identity.* Newark: University of Delaware Press, 2003.

Cooper, Wayne F. *Claude McKay, Rebel Sojourner in the Harlem Renaissance: A Biography.* Baton Rouge: Louisiana State University Press, 1996.

Corcoran, Neil. "Seamus Heaney and the Art of the Exemplary." *Yearbook of English Studies* 17 (1987): 117–27.

Cort, David. "Democracy, Unlimited: Hitler Talks of His 'New Revolution' but America Says It's Tyranny and to Hell with It." *Life,* August 19, 1940, 70.

Costello, Bonnie. *The Plural of Us: Poetry and Community in Auden and Others.* Princeton, NJ: Princeton University Press, 2007.

Crick, John. *Robert Lowell.* Edinburgh: Oliver and Boyd, 1974.

Culler, Jonathan. "Poésie et cliché Chez Baudelaire." In *Le Cliché,* edited by Gilles Mathis, 205–17. Toulouse: Presses Universitaires du Mirail, 1998.

"Curran Demands End of 'Red Threat': Urges Republican Victory as Only Way to Put Down Communism in U.S." *New York Times,* November 5, 1944, 43.

Dallek, Robert. *Lone Star Rising.* Vol. 1 of *Lyndon Johnson and His Times, 1908–1960.* New York: Oxford University Press, 1991.

Davie, Donald. *Purity of Diction in English Verse.* London: Routledge, 1967.

Deer, Patrick. "Auden and Wars." In *W. H. Auden in Context,* edited by Tony Sharpe, 150–59. Cambridge: Cambridge University Press, 2013.

Dickey, James. "Randall Jarrell." In *Randall Jarrell, 1914–1965,* edited by Robert Lowell, Peter Taylor, and Robert Penn Warren, 33–48. New York: Farrar, Straus and Giroux, 1967.

Dinsman, Melissa. *Modernism at the Microphone: Radio, Propaganda, and Literary Aesthetics during World War II.* London: Bloomsbury, 2015.

Doreski, William. *The Years of Our Friendship: Robert Lowell and Allen Tate.* Jackson: University Press of Mississippi, 1990.

Douglass, Frederick. "The Color Line." *North American Review* 132 (1881): 567–77.

Du Bois, W. E. B. "Criteria of Negro Art." In *The New Negro: Readings on Race, Representation, and African American Culture, 1892–1938,* edited by Henry Louis Gates Jr. and Gene Andrew Jarrett, 257–60. Princeton, NJ: Princeton University Press, 2007.

———. Review of *Home to Harlem,* by Claude McKay. *Crisis* 35 (1928): 202.

Eliot, T. S. *Collected Poems and Plays.* London: Faber and Faber, 1969.

"Excerpts from Johnson Vietnam Speech." *New York Times,* May 18, 1966.

Facos, Michelle. *An Introduction to Nineteenth-Century Art.* New York: Routledge, 2011.

Farber, David. *The Age of Great Dreams: America in the 1960s.* New York: Hill and Wang, 1994.

Feiler, Arthur. *The Experiment of Bolshevism.* London: Allen and Unwin, 1939.

Fein, Richard. "Randall Jarrell's World of War." In *Critical Essays on Randall Jarrell,* edited by Suzanne Ferguson, 149–62. Boston: G. K. Hall, 1983.

Feldman, Matthew. *Ezra Pound's Fascist Propaganda, 1935–45.* Basingstoke, UK: Palgrave, 2013.

Ferber, Michael. *Dictionary of Literary Symbols.* Cambridge: Cambridge University Press, 2007.

Ferguson, Suzanne. *The Poetry of Randall Jarrell.* Baton Rouge: Louisiana State University Press, 1971.

Finchow, Peter Edgerly. *W. H. Auden: Contexts for Poetry.* Newark: University of Delaware Press, 2002.

Flamm, Michael W., and David Steigerwald. *Debating the 1960s: Liberal, Conservative, and Radical Perspectives.* Lanham, MD: Rowman and Littlefield, 2008.

Foster, Thomas C. *Seamus Heaney.* Boston: Twayne, 1989.

"Four Freedoms." Washington, DC: Office of War Information, 1943.

Friedlander, Benjamin. "The Best Years of Our Lives: Randall Jarrell's War Poetry." In *Reading the Middle Generation Anew: Culture, Community and Form in Twentieth-Century Poetry,* edited by Eric Haralson, 83–112. Iowa City: University of Iowa Press, 2006.

Frost, Robert. *The Poetry of Robert Frost.* Edited by Edward Connery Lathem. New York: Henry Holt, 1979.

Fuller, John. *W. H. Auden: A Commentary*. Princeton, NJ: Princeton University Press, 2000.

Fussell, Paul. *Wartime: Understanding and Behavior in the Second World War*. Oxford: Oxford University Press, 1989.

Gardella, Peter. *American Civil Religion: What Americans Hold Sacred*. New York: Oxford University Press, 2013.

Gibson, Richelle. "This Week's Personality." *Saturday Review,* April 19, 1951, 60–65.

Gillette John Morris, and James Melvin Reinhardt. *Current Social Problems*. New York: American Book Company, 1933.

Goldensohn, Lorrie. *Dismantling Glory: Twentieth-Century Soldier Poetry*. New York: Columbia University Press, 2013.

Goldsmith, Kenneth. *Seven American Deaths and Disasters*. New York: powerHouse, 2013.

———. *Uncreative Writing*. New York: Columbia University Press, 2011.

Graham, Jorie. *Overlord*. New York: HarperCollins, 2005.

Graham, W. S. "It All Comes Back to Me Now." *Poetry* 72, no. 6 (September 1948): 302–7.

Gramsci, Antonio. *Selections from Prison Notebooks*. Edited and translated by Quintin Hoare and Geoffrey Nowell Smith. New York: International, 1971.

Green, Fiona. "Locating the Lyric: Marianne Moore, Elizabeth Bishop and the Second World War." In *Locations of Literary Modernism: Region and Nation in British and American Modernist Poetry,* edited by Alex Davis and Lee M. Jenkins, 199–214. Cambridge: Cambridge University Press, 2000.

Griffin, Barbara J. "Claude McKay: The Evolution of a Conservative." *CLA Journal* 36, no. 2 (December 1992): 157–70.

Hamilton, Ian. *Robert Lowell: A Biography*. New York: Random House, 1982.

"Harrison Says Go On: He Speaks at the Paris Banquet on Expansion." *Washington Post,* July 5, 1899.

Hayes, Terrance. *Lighthead*. New York: Penguin, 2010.

Heaney, Seamus. *Crediting Poetry: The Nobel Lecture*. New York: Farrar, Straus and Giroux, 2014.

———. *Death of a Naturalist*. London: Faber and Faber, 1966.

———. *North*. London: Faber and Faber, 1975.

———. *The Redress of Poetry*. New York: Farrar, Straus and Giroux, 1996.

Hecht, Anthony. *The Hidden Law: The Poetry of W. H. Auden*. Cambridge, MA: Harvard University Press, 1993.

Horten, Gerd. *Radio Goes to War: The Cultural Politics of Propaganda during World War II*. Berkeley: University of California Press, 2002.

Hughes, Langston. "Art and Integrity." *Chicago Defender,* October 20, 1945.

———. *The Collected Poems of Langston Hughes.* Edited by Arnold Rampersad. New York: Vintage, 1994.

———. *I Wonder as I Wander: An Autobiographical Journey.* New York: Farrar, Straus and Giroux, 2015.

James, William. *Essays in Religion and Morality.* Vol. 9 of *The Works of William James,* edited by Frederick Burkhardt and John Joseph McDermott. Cambridge, MA: Harvard University Press, 1982.

Jarrell, Randall. "Changes of Attitude and Rhetoric in Auden's Poetry." *Southern Review* 7, no. 2 (Autumn 1941): 326–49.

———. *The Complete Poems.* New York: Farrar, Straus and Giroux, 1981.

———. *Kipling, Auden & Co.* New York: Farrar, Straus and Giroux, 1980.

———. *Randall Jarrell's Letters: An Autobiographical and Literary Selection.* Edited by Mary Jarrell. Wilmington, MA: Houghton Mifflin, 1985.

Johnson, Lyndon B. *Public Papers of the Presidents of the United States: Lyndon B. Johnson, 1965.* Washington, DC: Federal Register Division, National Archives and Records Service, General Services Administration, 1966.

Johnston, Dillon. *Irish Poetry after Joyce.* Syracuse, NY: Syracuse University Press, 1997.

Jung, Carl. *Psychology and Religion.* New Haven, CT: Yale University Press, 1938.

Kierkegaard, Soren. *The Living Thoughts of Kierkegaard.* New York: David McKay, 1952.

Koch, Kenneth. *New Addresses.* New York: Knopf, 2000.

Kutzinski, Vera M. *The Worlds of Langston Hughes: Modernism and Translation in the Americas.* Ithaca, NY: Cornell University Press, 2012.

Lindeman, Eduard C., and Clyde R. Miller. Introduction to *War Propaganda and the United States,* edited by Harold Lavine and James Wechsler. New Haven, CT: Yale University Press, 1940.

Lippmann, Walter. "The All-Purpose Myth." *Newsweek,* May 24, 1965.

Longley, Edna. "Fire and Air." *Honest Ulsterman* 50 (winter 1975): 179–83.

———. *Poetry in the Wars.* Newark: University of Delaware Press, 1987.

Lowell, Robert. *Collected Poems.* Edited by Frank Bidart and David Gewanter. New York: Farrar, Straus and Giroux, 2007.

———. *Collected Prose.* Edited by Robert Giroux. New York: Farrar, Straus and Giroux, 1990.

Lutz, William. *Doublespeak: From "Revenue Enhancement" to "Terminal Living."* New York: Harper and Row, 1987.

Lynch, Timothy. "Doublespeak and the War on Terrorism." *Cato Institute Briefing Papers* 98 (September 6, 2006).

Marcuse, Herbert. *One-Dimensional Man.* Boston: Beacon, 1964.

McKay, Claude. *Complete Poems.* Edited by William J. Maxwell. Champaign: University of Illinois Press, 2004.

———. *A Long Way from Home.* Edited by Gene Andrew Jarrett. New Brunswick, NJ: Rutgers University Press, 2007.

———. "The Negro Writer to His Critics." In *The New Negro: Readings on Race, Representation, and African American Culture, 1892–1938,* edited by Henry Louis Gates Jr. and Gene Andrew Jarrell, 390–94. Princeton, NJ: Princeton University Press, 2007.

———. *The Passion of Claude McKay: Selected Poetry and Prose, 1912–1948.* Edited by Wayne F. Cooper. New York: Schocken, 1973.

———. "Soviet Russia and the Negro." *Crisis,* December 1923, 61–65.

McLaren, Joseph. *Langston Hughes, Folk Dramatist in the Protest Tradition, 1921–1943.* Westport, CT: Greenwood, 1997.

Mendelson, Edward. *Early Auden, Later Auden: A Critical Biography.* Princeton, NJ: Princeton University Press, 2017.

Miles, Josephine. *Civil Poems.* Berkeley, CA: Oyez, 1966.

———. *Collected Poems: 1930–83.* Urbana: University of Illinois Press, 1983.

———. *The Continuity of Poetic Language.* New York: Octagon, 1965.

———. *Fields of Learning.* Berkeley, CA: Oyez, 1968.

———. *Kinds of Affection.* Middletown, CT: Wesleyan University Press, 1967.

Moore, Marianne. *New Collected Poems.* Edited by Heather Cass White. New York: Farrar, Straus and Giroux, 2017.

Morin Rebecca, and David Cohen. "Giuliani: 'Truth Isn't Truth.'" *Politico,* August 19, 2018. https://www.politico.com/story/2018/08/19/giuliani-truth-todd-trump-788161.

Morrison, Samuel Eliot. *The Oxford History of the American People.* New York: Oxford University Press, 1965.

Muller, Erik. *Josephine Miles.* Boise, ID: Boise State University Press, 2005.

Murphy, Andrew. *Seamus Heaney.* London: Northcote House, 2000.

Murphy, Michael. "Neoclassicism, Late Modernism, and W. H. Auden's 'New Year Letter.'" *Cambridge Quarterly* 33, no. 2 (2004): 101–18.

Nash, Ogden. "My Victory Garden." *Home & Garden,* November 1943.

Nemerov, Howard. *The Collected Poems of Howard Nemerov*. Chicago: University of Chicago Press, 2015.

———. *War Stories: Poems about Long Ago and Now*. Chicago: University of Chicago Press, 1990.

Nordström, Folke. *Goya, Saturn, and Melancholy: Studies in the Art of Goya*. Stockholm: Almqvist and Wiksell, 1962.

North, Jessica Nelson. "Josephine Miles." In *Trial Balances*, edited by Ann Winslow, 23–24. New York: Macmillan, 1935.

O'Driscoll, Dennis. "Heaney in Public." In *The Cambridge Companion to Seamus Heaney*, edited by Bernard O'Donoghue, 56–72. Cambridge: Cambridge University Press, 2009.

Oostdijk, Diederik. *Among the Nightmare Fighters: American Poets of World War II*. Columbia: University of South Carolina Press, 2011.

Orwell, George. *Essays*. London: Penguin, 2000.

———. "Political Reflections on the Crisis." *Adelphi*, December 1938.

Paine, Thomas. *Rights of Man, Common Sense, and Other Political Writings*. Edited by Mark Philip. Oxford: Oxford University Press, 1995.

Pei, Mario. *Doublespeak in America*. New York: Hawthorn, 1973.

Pritchard, William H. *Randall Jarrell: A Literary Life*. New York: Farrar, Straus and Giroux, 1990.

Ramazani, Jahan. *Poetry of Mourning: The Modern Elegy from Hardy to Heaney*. Chicago: University of Chicago Press, 1994.

Rampersad, Arnold. *The Life of Langston Hughes*. 2 vols. Oxford: Oxford University Press, 1986–2002.

Randall, John Herman. *A World Community: The Supreme Task of the Twentieth Century*. New York: Frederick A. Stokes, 1930.

Rawson, Hugh. *A Dictionary of Euphemisms & Other Doubletalk*. New York: Crown, 1981.

Roosevelt, Franklin D. *Franklin Delano Roosevelt: Great Speeches*. Edited by John Grafton. New York: Dover, 1999.

Ricks, Christopher. *The Force of Poetry*. Oxford, UK: Clarendon, 1984.

Russell, Richard Rankin. *Poetry and Peace: Michael Longley, Seamus Heaney, and Northern Ireland*. Notre Dame, IN: University of Notre Dame Press, 2010.

Safire, William. *Safire's Political Dictionary*. New York: Oxford University Press, 2008.

Schulze, Robin. "How Not to Edit: The Case of Marianne Moore." *Textual Cultures: Texts, Contexts, Interpretation* 2, no. 1 (spring 2007): 119–35.

Schweik, Susan. *A Gulf So Deeply Cut: American Women Poets and the Second World War.* Madison: University of Wisconsin Press, 1991.

Shiach, Morag. "'To Purify the Dialect of the Tribe': Modernism and Language Reform." *Modernism/modernity* 14, no. 1 (January 2007): 21–34.

Shoptaw, John. *On the Outside Looking Out.* Cambridge, MA: Harvard University Press, 1994.

Spargo, R. Clifton. *The Ethics of Mourning: Grief and Responsibility in Elegiac Literature.* Baltimore: Johns Hopkins University Press, 2004.

Spiegelman, Willard. *The Didactic Muse: Scenes of Instruction in Contemporary American Poetry.* Princeton, NJ: Princeton University Press, 1989.

Steinman, Lisa M. "Putting on Knowledge with Power: The Poetry of Josephine Miles." *Chicago Review* 37, no. 1 (winter 1990): 130–40.

Summer, Judith. *Plants Go to War: A Botanical History of World War II.* Jefferson, NC: McFarland, 2019.

Swift, Jonathan. *The Essential Writings: Authoritative Texts, Contexts, Criticism.* Edited by Claude Julien Rawson and Ian Higgins. New York: Norton, 2010.

Terkel, Studs. *The Good War: An Oral History of World War II.* New York: Pantheon, 1984.

"Text of Eisenhower's Speech on the Mutual Security Program." *New York Times,* May 3, 1960.

"Text of Herbert Hoover's Address on 'the Question of Peace.'" *New York Times,* March 29, 1941.

"Text of Johnson's Address to A.P. on Nuclear Cuts and U.S. Foreign Policy." *New York Times,* April 21, 1964.

"Text of Kennedy's Address to the Nation on His Talks in Europe." *New York Times,* June 7, 1961.

"Text of Truman's Speech Telling of U.S. Fight on Communists." *New York Times,* April 25, 1940.

"Text of Wicks' Keynote Address to G.O.P." *New York Times,* September 7, 1950.

Tillery, Tyrone. *Claude McKay: A Black Poet's Struggle for Identity.* Amherst: University of Massachusetts Press, 1992.

Tobin, Daniel. *Passage to the Center: Imagination and the Sacred in the Poetry of Seamus Heaney.* Lexington: University Press of Kentucky, 1999.

Trilling, Lionel. *The Liberal Imagination.* New York: New York Review of Books, 2008.

Vendler, Helen. *Part of Nature, Part of Us: Modern American Poets.* Cambridge, MA: Harvard University Press, 1980.

———. "A Quarter of Poetry." Review of *To All Appearances: Poems New and Selected,* by Josephine Miles. *New York Times,* April 6, 1975.

Wagner, Jean. *Black Poets of the United States: From Paul Laurence Dunbar to Langston Hughes.* Champaign: University of Illinois Press, 1973.

Wall, Wendy L. *Inventing the "American Way": The Politics of Consensus from the New Deal to the Civil Rights Movement.* Oxford: Oxford University Press, 2009.

Warner, Michael. "Publics and Counterpublics." *Public Culture* 14, no. 1 (2002): 49–90.

Wasley, Aidan. *The Age of Auden: Postwar Poetry and the American Scene.* Princeton, NJ: Princeton University Press, 2011.

Watson, Don. *Death Sentences: How Clichés, Weasel Words, and Management-Speak Are Strangling Public Language.* New York: Gotham, 2005.

Weatherson Michael A., and Hal W. Bochin. *Hiram Johnson: Political Revivalist.* Boston: United Press of America, 1995.

Winkler, Allan M. *The Politics of Propaganda: The Office of War Information, 1942–1945.* New Haven, CT: Yale University Press, 1978.

Women in Defense. Directed by John Ford. Office for Emergency Management, 1941.

Wordsworth, William. *The Major Works.* Edited by Stephen Gill. Oxford: Oxford University Press, 1984.

Yeats, W. B. *Yeats' Poems.* Edited by A. Norman Jeffares. Houndmills, UK: Macmillan, 1996.

INDEX

CPSIA information can be obtained
at www.ICGtesting.com
Printed in the USA
LVHW042304200423
744981LV00001B/42